Keys to Inspiration

Keys to Inspiration

A Teacher's Guide to a Student-Centered Writing Program

Steve Ford

ROWMAN & LITTLEFIELD
Lanham • Boulder • New York • London

Published by Rowman & Littlefield
An imprint of The Rowman & Littlefield Publishing Group, Inc.
4501 Forbes Boulevard, Suite 200, Lanham, Maryland 20706
www.rowman.com

Unit A, Whitacre Mews, 26-34 Stannary Street, London SE11 4AB

Copyright © 2018 by Steve Ford

All rights reserved. No part of this book may be reproduced in any form or by any electronic or mechanical means, including information storage and retrieval systems, without written permission from the publisher, except by a reviewer who may quote passages in a review.

British Library Cataloguing in Publication Information Available

Library of Congress Cataloging-in-Publication Data Available

ISBN 978-1-4758-3872-5 (hardback : alk. paper) | ISBN 978-1-4758-3873-2 (pbk. : alk. paper) | ISBN 978-1-4758-3874-9 (ebook)

∞ ™ The paper used in this publication meets the minimum requirements of American National Standard for Information Sciences Permanence of Paper for Printed Library Materials, ANSI/NISO Z39.48-1992.

Printed in the United States of America

Contents

Foreword: A Maple Syrup Book: Sweet Wisdom for Every Writing Teacher	xiii
Preface	xv
Acknowledgments	xix
Introduction	xxi
Notes	xxii

Section I: Let's Write! 1

1 Moment One, Day One— Taking the Plunge	3
What You Need to Know	3
What You Need to Do	4
Option	5
2 Revising Moment One: Questions in the Margins	7
What You Need to Know	7
What You Need to Do	8
Day 1	10
Day 2	11
Day 3	12
Day 4	12
3 Student Biographies	13
What You Need to Know	13
What You Need to Do	15
Day 1	17
Day 2	18
Day 3	18

	Day 4	18
	Day 5	19
	Option	19
	Note	20
4	Respect, the Booklet	21
	What You Need to Know	21
	What You Need to Do	22
	Day 1	23
	Day 2	24
	Day 3 (or 4)	24
	Options	25
5	Writers' Workshop	27
6	Assessment	31
	What You Need to Know	31
	What You Need to Do	32
	Note	35
7	Commonalities: General to Specific	37
	What You Need to Know	37
	Specific Commonalities	38
	What You Need to Do	39
	Final Note	40
8	Dramatic Details	41
	What You Need to Know	41
	What You Need to Do	42
	Homework	42
	Activity 1	42
	Activity 2	43
	Activity 3	43
	Activity 4	43
	Activity 5	43
	Options	44
9	Odd Objects	45
	What You Need to Know	46
	What You Need to Do	46
	Activity 1	46
	Activity 2	48
	Option	48
10	Music Picture/Writing	49
	What You Need to Know	49
	What You Need to Do	50
	Day 1	50

Day 2	51
Day 3	51
Option	52
11 A Non-Essay on Elements	**53**
What You Need to Know	53
What You Need to Do	54
Day 1	54
Day 2	55
Options	55
12 Slow Motion	**57**
What You Need to Know	58
Example 1	58
Example 2	58
What You Need to Do	58
Suggested Triggers	59
13 Fast-Forward	**61**
What You Need to Know	62
What You Need to Do	62
Life Segments That Might Resonate with Students	63
14 Create a Life	**65**
What You Need to Know	65
What You Need to Do	66
Options	66
15 Let's Write a Walter Mitty!	**67**
What You Need to Know	67
What You Need to Do	68
What to Expect from Your Storytellers	69
Inspiration	69
16 In Other Words: Paraphrasing	**71**
What You Need to Know	71
What You Need to Do	72
Day 1	73
Days 2 and 3	74
Days 4 and 5: Showtime	74
Options	74
Suggested Documents for Paraphrasing	74
17 Write More!: Things to Consider	**77**
Poetry	77
Folktales	78
Suggested Titles for Made-Up Folktales	79
Cartoons	79

Homograph Stories	80
Some Things Are Analogous; Some Are Not	80
I Hear Your Voice!	80
Create an Island of Propriety	81

Section II: Major Projects — 83

18 Commonalities in Essays, Editorials, Research Writing, and Debate: An Introduction to Four Projects — 85

19 Persuasive Essay — 89
- What You Need to Know — 91
- What You Need to Do — 91
  - Day 1 — 91
  - Day 2 — 92
  - Day 3 — 92

20 Editorials and Editorial Cartoons — 93
- What You Need to Know — 93
- What You Need to Do — 94
  - Day 1 — 96
  - Day 2 — 98
  - Day 3 — 98
  - Day 4 — 99
  - Day 5 — 100
  - Options — 101

21 Writing a Research Report — 103
- What You Need to Know — 103
- What You Need to Do — 104
  - Some Tips about Note Taking and Structure — 105
- Sample Research Report — 107
- Note — 111

22 Debate — 113
- What You Need to Know — 113
- What You Need to Do — 114
  - Two Weeks before You Want the Debates to Start — 115
  - The Next Day — 115
  - Day 1 (Three to Six Days before the First Debates) — 116
  - Day 2 — 116
  - Day 3 — 117
  - Days 4, 5, and 6 (for older students) — 117
  - Options — 117

23 Oral Presentations — 119
- What You Need to Know — 119

What You Need to Do	120
Inventions	123
How Things Work	123
Hobbies and the Arts	124
Unusual Animals	124
Biology	124
History	124
People	125
Inventors and Scientists	125
Disasters	125
Great Accomplishments	125
24 Technical Writing	127
What You Need to Know	128
What You Need to Do	128
Day 1	128
Day 2	129
Options	129
Section III: Mechanics	**131**
25 Introduction to Mechanics	133
26 Grammar	139
Irregular Verb Tenses: A Good Place to Start	140
Subject–Verb Agreement	143
Troublesome Subject–Verb Agreement	143
Who or Whom	144
Pronouns That Precede Which, Whom, and Whose	144
Parallel Structure	145
Coordinate Adjectives and Those That Are Not	146
Adjectives Ending in -*ly* That Are Mistaken for Adverbs	146
Misplaced Modifiers	147
Misplaced Adverbs	148
27 Punctuation, Clauses, and Sentence Types	149
Clauses	149
Sentences	150
The Four Types of Sentences	150
The Four Moods of Sentences	150
End Marks	151
The Period (.)	151
The Question Mark (?)	151
The Exclamation Mark/Point (!)	152
In-between Marks	152
The Comma (,)	152

Quotation Marks (" ")	155
The Semicolon (;)	157
What You Need to Know	158
What You Need to Do	159
The Apostrophe (')	159
The Ellipsis (. . .)	160
The Hyphen (-)	161
The Dash (—)	162
The Colon (:)	162
Parentheses ( )	163
28 Spelling	165
What You Need to Know	166
What You Need to Do	166
Section IV: Appendixes	**171**
Appendix A: Spelling Lists	173
Long *A* (a_e, ea, ai, ei, ay, ey, eigh)	173
Aw as in Saw (aw, au, ough, augh)	174
Er (B<u>er</u>t's b<u>ir</u>d b<u>ur</u>ps <u>wor</u>ms <u>ear</u>ly; er, ir, ur, wor, ear)	174
Long *E* (ē, e_e, ee, ea, ie, ei, ey)	175
Long *O* (ō, o_e, ou, oe, oa, ough, ow, oo)	176
Long *I* (ī, i_e, y, ei, igh)	176
Ow as in Cloud (ou, ough, ow)	177
Sh and Zh Words	178
Appendix B: Spelling-Related Lists	179
Silent Letters	179
Groups of Confusing Spellings	180
Words Ending in *L*	183
Rule 10 Words	185
Latin and Greek Roots	186
Mispronounced, Thus Misspelled, Words	189
Curious Spelling Changes from One Word Form to Another	190
Appendix C: Other Lists	193
Conjunctive Adverbs and Transitional Phrases	193
Emotional Events	194
Emotions and Emotion-Related Words	195
Nouns	195
Verbs	196
Facial Expressions	196
Facial Features, Hands	197
Eyes Can Appear . . .	197

Faces Can Appear . . .	197
Noses Can Be . . .	198
Complexion Can Be . . .	198
Hands/Fingers Can Appear . . .	198
Homographs	199
Idioms, Sayings, Expressions	200
Irregular Verbs	202
Moral/Ethical Vocabulary	203
Nouns	203
Adjectives	204
Verbs	204
Multiple-Meaning Words	205
Powerful Verbs	206
Other Ways to Say "Went"	206
Other Ways to Say "Said"	208
Persuasive Essay Topics	209
Kids Philosophy Slam Topics	209
Author-Generated Topics	209
Bibliography	211

Foreword

A Maple Syrup Book:
Sweet Wisdom for Every Writing Teacher

In their inspirational book about reading instruction *Disrupting Thinking*, Kylene Beers and Bob Probst create a useful three-step paradigm that teachers can use to create deeper readers:

Book
Head
Heart

Book—What the words say. What happened.
Head—What you think about what the words say.
Heart—What wisdom you take away from reading this book.

Most reading tests measure only the first step, what happened in the book. The other two steps happen in the classrooms of skilled teachers who give students the light and space to find out what they really think and how it changes how they see the world.

Writing instruction can be just as transformational when teachers go beyond formulaic instruction and help their students put their thoughts and their hearts on the page. This type of teaching is an art that can never be automated. Software-driven classrooms may be the dream of tech billionaires, but all we need to do is think of a teacher who changed our own lives to see the truth. Rarely do we think of what they taught us, but rather, as Maya Angelou said, "We remember how they made us feel," how they listened to our ideas and gave us the confidence to discover what we really think. Great writing teachers give students the tools and craft to find their own wisdom and to believe in their own learning.

Keys to Inspiration: A Teacher's Guide to a Student-Centered Writing Program by Steve Ford is a book jam-packed with years of boiled-down wisdom from such a life-changing teacher.

In his preface, Ford talks about connecting students to their own emotional life:

> What I quickly came to realize was that emotion is not simply an ingredient in a writing recipe; it is, in fact, inspiration itself, and it has been since language emerged. Indeed, it probably inspired the very idea of language! That day, before the term was coined, I began to appreciate the meaning of "student-centered" learning. We hear it a lot these days, but only when we allow students to write from the heart do we begin to deliver on that implied promise.

A wise sage once said, "A strong horse will pull any cart." This inspirational teaching guide will show you how to unbridle all the wild horses in your students' writing hearts. Use the simple exercises Ford has developed over years of teaching, and take note of all the practical tools he gives you, from idea gathering to drafting, revising, crafting details, dialogue, grammar, editing, assessment, critical thinking, and more. But as you use this book to develop classes of student writers, don't be fooled into thinking this is just a textbook of remedial skills. Read closely and you will see that Ford has boiled down these ideas from years of teaching into a sweet syrup. You will taste the syrup and adapt its sweetness to your students. Under Ford's guidance, you will learn to give your students the tools and the space to be writers and thinkers. You will learn to hand students the keys to their own inspiration.

Barry Lane
author and teacher
DiscoverWriting.com

Preface

After I retired, I thought I would return to my own writing, but Edward Albee got in the way. A quote that's been attributed to him—"I write to find out what I'm thinking about"—hung in my classroom for years, and it followed me out the door. No matter what I did, I couldn't stop writing about writing.

A lot of it is driven by frustration with "the system." Everyone you talk to these days is lamenting the sorry state of writing in America. States are dropping proof of writing proficiency as a prerequisite for high school graduation. Essays are becoming optional for college applicants, even as those same colleges are establishing remedial writing labs. Employers are hiring outside consultants to tutor their employees. And now, finally, if you read and listen closely, you'll notice that the second R has been squeezed out of the national discussion by its partners on either side of it.

The sad thing is that, on its face, writing is not all that complicated; in fact, as I began this book, I came up with the idea of creating a "recipe for writing": combine a bunch of detail, some powerful verbs, a dash each of adjectives, adverbs, simile, and metaphor, simmer them slowly in a skillet, and—voilà—a delicious confit de verbiage! I soon realized, however, that I had a whole cookbook on my hands, and a heightened appreciation for the work of Julia Child.

What flummoxes us, though, is not the study of mechanics, or even the ethereal nature of its better half—content. It's that we don't understand why people write in the first place—we write, whether we're six or sixty, because we're *inspired*! But inspiration comes from within. It's not one of the standards that guides our curricula, and it isn't delivered via "helpful" writing prompts; when we tell students what to write about, we're really telling them what *we* might want to write about. So we have a problem: How do we get kids to "self-inspire"? How do we get them excited about required assignments?

Young writers are like oysters: sometimes we have to *irritate* them—coax them—into producing a "pearl." The process is a bit invasive, but the product can be quite lovely. Even so, there is something missing—*inspiration*—the natural catalyst that seems to come out of nowhere to compel an oyster or writer to produce something unique and, oh, so precious; unfortunately, neither the jewelry market nor our education system is patient enough to wait for pearls to drop, and that's where we teachers come in.

Let's face it: we're in the motivation business. It's our job to get kids to produce, to move them toward completion of a task and its ultimate reward—pride in accomplishment. We love it, of course, when our students are *self-*motivated; we simply assign a topic for an essay, a subject for a poem, or provide a "story starter," and then circulate around the room, nodding our approval as we look over their shoulders. This approach sometimes produces adequate results, but we're fooling ourselves if we think these students are self-motivated; more accurately, they're self-disciplined, and motivated more by a sense of duty than an irrepressible urge to craft something truly original. So, what's a teacher to do?

That's what I wondered as I struggled to find my way after I was put in charge of teaching 125 sixth graders to be better writers. I had no curriculum, and my passion for writing proved to be an inadequate substitute. One day, one of our student teachers dropped a copy of Barry Lane's book *After the End: Teaching and Learning Creative Revision* in my lap; she thought I'd "like it," and I did.

Mr. Lane's work was fresh. It actually focused on content, and it contained cool exercises. In one of them, students were instructed to describe, in detail, a place they knew well, but through the "filter" of an emotion. Excited, I tried it out on my kids, several of whom chose their bedroom as that special place. They wrote things like, "My dolls' eyes stared disapprovingly at me," and, "The sun's rays were like 'warm arrows' coming through my window." I was stunned; they were using words to convey emotions, but without identifying them by name.

What I quickly came to realize was that emotion is not simply an ingredient in a writing recipe; it is, in fact, inspiration itself, and it has been since language emerged. Indeed, it probably inspired the very idea of language! That day, before the term was coined, I began to appreciate the meaning of "student-centered" learning. We hear it a lot these days, but only when we allow students to write from the heart do we begin to deliver on that implied promise.

A good way to begin is demonstrated in chapter 1. The lesson is called "Moment One, Day One—Taking the Plunge," and it invites students to write about emotional experiences. You'll be excited to see the level of engagement, but there's something more important waiting: young writers who can bring themselves to write honestly—from their hearts—will express their writer's truth, and if they can muster the courage to share their stories, they'll be in line to receive affirmation from their peers and teacher, and gain the confidence to write more.

Connecting kids to writing through their emotions also helps to cure writer's block, that tired old term that should be renamed "insecurity." It's a disease that we catch when we're young, and it makes us stop believing in ourselves. We sit and stare and fail to think of anything to write, and we convince ourselves that no one will care about what we have to say. Well, Brenda Ueland taught us that "everyone has something important to say," and you need to pass that message on to your students. You need to tell them to stop straining their brains in an effort to "discover" something to write about and, instead, write what's in their hearts and trust their brains to follow, à la Edward Albee.

The lessons and projects contained in this book were designed to address both content and mechanics issues, and they reflect the highest academic standards. My hope is that you will find them useful and that students will find them fun and challenging. Our kids today are smarter than ever, and it's unacceptable that so many of them are struggling as writers. We all have to step up—training institutions, state departments of education, school districts, and individual teachers—and serve them better. They have a lot to say about their world, and it's up to us to nurture that voice.

Finally, like many of you, I was disappointed with the training I received; I persevered because I loved what I was doing. I was lucky to find Barry Lane, Frank McCourt, and Donald Graves to point me in the right direction, and, later, Brenda Ueland, Natalie Goldberg, Anne Lamott, and Annie Dillard, who affirmed what I was doing all along. May you learn as much from me as I did from them.

Acknowledgments

"The little things are bigger than you think" is an expression that writing teachers invoke as they coax their young scribes to express their thoughts. It's about convincing kids that they have important things to say about their world, and that good writing doesn't have to be large or loud; honest treatment of everyday experiences will suffice.

While many people helped me make this book a reality, most of them probably don't realize it. They are the countless parents and students who cheered me on, assuring me that I had something important to say about teaching writing, and that it needed to be heard.

I owe a big thank-you to Mary Dybvig, a principal who saw the wisdom of separating reading and writing instruction. This meant that my able partner, Debbie Wright, could focus on reading and children's literature, and I was free to develop a meaningful writing curriculum. Working together, we fed 125 sixth graders a double dose of language arts every day. I also have to recognize another colleague, Heather McKinley. As I was struggling to find ways to convert my passion for writing into a teaching strategy, she gave me a copy of Barry Lane's book *After the End: Teaching and Learning Creative Revision*. This "little thing" turned out to be a big influence on me, for Mr. Lane's refreshing focus on content completely changed my approach to teaching writing.

When I got serious about writing my own book, I reached out to friends and acquaintances in the business. Kate Hopper, author and creative writing teacher, looked at my first attempt at a book proposal, gave me some valuable feedback, and urged me to keep going. Then I ran into Laura Zats—a former student, no less—at an AWP (Association of Writers & Writing Programs) conference. When I learned she was an editor at Wise Ink Publications, the writing was on the wall. I asked her to work with me on my proposal, and she jumped at the chance to reverse our roles and "tear it apart." This book is evidence that she did a great job. My friend Peggy Johnson, author of library science textbooks, also helped me with my proposal by showing me how to search for competing titles. Peter C. Brown, another friend and author, gave me the gift of faith, for after I shared my first chapters with him he affirmed my work and made me believe it was worthy of publication.

Thanks also to the many teachers I worked with over the years, as well as those who read sample chapters and provided honest feedback—notably Mary Haug, my son's former English teacher extraordinaire, upon whom I leaned heavily. Book and paper artist Steve Pittelkow deserves special mention for helping my students with their end-of-year, handmade book projects; their pride in accomplishment was his only reward.

I also want to thank my editors at Rowman & Littlefield—Tom Koerner for believing in me and helping me find my technical voice, and Carlie Wall for patiently answering my myriad questions. Lawyers, too, come in handy sometimes, and mine, Dan Satorius, took a load off my shoulders by negotiating a fair book contract. Thanks, Dan.

Finally, after enduring years of listening to me talk about how the world needed this book, my family jumped at the chance to push me across the finish line. My son, Alex, a superb math teacher, offered constructive criticism; my daughter and gifted artist, Elizabeth, agreed to create a few lovely illustrations; but my wife, Beth, a computer wiz, is the reason this book was completed. She organized and formatted my written ramblings, kept me calm, and got it done. Thank you, dear.

Introduction

If any academic discipline fits the definition of holistic, it's writing. It could also be said that a piece of writing, as a whole, is greater than the sum of its parts. It's even holistic on a micro level: every paragraph supports the overall content, and each sentence demands good mechanics skills, an understanding of all of the parts of speech, and a rich vocabulary; in other words, writing cannot be taught piecemeal—everyone has to be all in, ideally on the first day of school.

Accordingly, the first chapter of Section I, "Moment One, Day One—Taking the Plunge," tosses students into the deep end. It asks each of them to write a detailed description of an emotional moment from his or her past, which eventually becomes the basis for a memoir. The second chapter, "Revising Moment One: Questions in the Margins," follows up with instructions for finishing it.

The third and fourth chapters, "Student Biographies" and "Respect, the Booklet," are also well suited for the beginning of the school year, as they help students get to know one another and establish healthy social behavior.

While the first four chapters demonstrate the importance of writing every day, as well as the connection between emotion and inspiration, chapters 5 through 7 focus on the teacher. They describe a well-managed writing classroom, provide tips on assessing student work, and reveal the elements that many forms of writing have in common—a valuable bit of knowledge that students can apply as they move from one project to another.

The remainder of Section I is devoted to a wide array of writing exercises. This is where young writers practice the all-important skill of conveying detail, experiment with a couple of handy writers' devices, and continue to recognize emotion as a presence in written work. These lessons can be taught in any order—teachers know best when to schedule projects within the ebb and flow of a school year.

Section II is intense, varied, rich in content, and rewarding. These projects—essay, editorial, research report, and debate—represent significant time spent researching, preparing, and presenting, so it's best to schedule them midyear or soon after. At that point, students will have acquired many of the skills they'll need to handle the work, but there'll be enough time left in the year to accomplish it.[1]

Section III is all about grammar, punctuation, and spelling. It serves as a teacher's guide to mechanics—featuring rules and examples—but also highlights the areas that are most problematic for young writers.

The appendixes contain unique word lists that teachers can refer to or download from the publisher. They include spelling lists to be handed out to students, lists to post in the classroom for student reference, and those, such as emotion and emotion-related word lists, that teachers can draw from to help students prepare for some of the lessons contained in this book.

Finally, there is one very important subject that's not assigned a chapter between these covers: call it "student-choice writing" or, as this author prefers, "open topic" writing. We need to provide developing writers the time and space to experiment with stories, essays, and poetry. Many of them will spend time writing at home, but they should also be allowed time to work on these personal projects in class. Open topic writing is not to be confused with "free writing" or journaling, neither of which requires form or finishing; these creative efforts should be completed, edited, proofread, and published—as either a portfolio or a handmade book—at year's end, and factored into final grades.[2]

This book contains several references to lesson-related materials that are available for download from the publisher's website, such as figures, tools, examples of various forms of writing, spelling tests, worksheets, and much more. Also available are almost all of the lists in the appendixes. These resources can be found on the *Keys to Inspiration* book page at https://rowman.com/ISBN/9781475838725/Keys-to-Inspiration-A-Teacher's-Guide-to-a-Student-Centered-Writing-Program. Once there, you will find what you need on the Features tab.

NOTES

1. This book was designed to be a guide for teachers of all grade levels; however, students' maturity and skill levels might call for adapting certain exercises, lessons, and projects, or even skipping a few.

2. Open topic writing should start at the beginning of the year and be treated as an essential part of your writing program.

Section I

Let's Write!

Chapter One

Moment One, Day One— Taking the Plunge

> *I must start out with an emotion—one that's close to me and that I can understand.*—F. Scott Fitzgerald

If writing teachers were more like those daring parents who teach their children to swim by throwing them into the deep end of a pool, they would schedule this project for the first day of school. The craft of writing is complicated, but it's foolish to isolate and teach its myriad skills one at a time, and out of context—better to make students dive in and learn fast.

The assignment Moment One sets the pace and expectations for the year, and it teaches young writers that they can revise, edit, and proofread with help from their peers. Most important, though, they learn that if they are emotionally inspired they'll take ownership of their written work and strive to improve it—all of us learn to be better writers by studying our own work.

WHAT YOU NEED TO KNOW

- Content is everything. If you prove to your students that they're capable of producing work that "moves" their classmates and garners positive feedback, you will have instilled in them a degree of confidence, and they'll be halfway home. (The rest of the trip is mechanics, but that will follow.)
- A tenet of this book is that emotion and inspiration are one and the same, and this assignment is designed to demonstrate that notion as it progresses from a simple exercise to a lovely memoir.
- Students, like many of us, don't think they have anything important to say. You'll be asking them to dredge up emotional memories, but some will

think theirs aren't worthy of an audience. Your job is to convince them that it's not about earth-shattering events; it's in the telling—the genuineness, the details, and the thoughts. (You'll run up against this "complex" again, so start discrediting it on day one.)
- Much of this first day will be taken up with brainstorming and discussion, so count on another period of in-class writing before moving on to the revision process along with some sharing of student work.
- You should expect the completed memoirs to be one and one-half to two and one-half typed pages in length.

WHAT YOU NEED TO DO

- Study the list of emotion and emotion-related words in appendix C and jot down any more that you think of.
- On day one, ask your students to think about the word *emotion* and its synonym, *feeling*. Inform them that they're about to begin a writing project that will involve emotions, but for now you just want them to come up with all the emotion words they can think of so you can record them (projected for viewing or scribbled on the board). Open your mind to their offerings: some emotion words are unambiguous (love, hate, joy, sadness), but others—those referred to above as emotion-related—might be just as evocative; for example, a word like *caring* might spark a memory of caring for an elderly family member who is approaching the end of his life—an emotional event indeed. (Remember, you'll be asking them to recall an episode from their past that was very emotional, so however they arrive at one is irrelevant.)
- When you've withdrawn everything from their "emotion banks," stand back and hold a brief discussion about the words displayed before them. (This is your time to add any that you think might be good candidates.) Then ask your students to imagine what situations might cause these emotions, and discuss them briefly.
- Tell your students to think about a time when they experienced one of these emotions—what caused the emotion, the people involved, and how it played out.

Note: It's important for students to select an event that occurred as far into the past as possible (at least several months, but preferably years). Moment One is going to be turned into a memoir, so it's essential that they be able to reflect on this experience from a distance and consider how it affected them. (For now, though, don't mention the memoir aspect.)

- Tell your budding memoirists that they need to pick a moment that they experienced with at least one other person. (This is necessary in order to make a specific revision explained in the next chapter, "Revising Moment One." If a student asks if the other "person" can be a pet, say no.)
- Finally, set them writing. Emphasize the need for vivid description as they recall the event—things their five senses picked up and details about actions, people, setting, and thoughts. Inform them that they'll have one more day of writing time (day two) and that the revision process will happen on days three and four.

Note: There's an intimate connection between the brain, the hand, and the pencil. Writing is messy, both literally and figuratively, and children need the freedom to scribble sentences, cross them out, write notes in the margins, draw arrows, and erase things. This writer strongly believes that electronic devices and pens are best left for final drafts, when creations are whole.

OPTION

While your students are writing, sit down and record a recollection of your own. That way, when the revision process starts, you can participate as a "student" and establish yourself as a role model. They'll love it.

Chapter Two

Revising Moment One

Questions in the Margins

Now that you've hooked your students on writing from the heart, they're a bit closer to discovering their writer's truth; sensing this, they'll be willing to invest time improving their Moment Ones and turning them into mini-memoirs. With help from their teacher and peers, they'll add that layer of detail that's often missing in the work of young writers, and they'll begin to learn what experienced writers seem to know instinctively—that the *details* described by the five senses, the *thoughts* of characters, and the *emotions* that direct the action are all necessary to a reader's experience.

When Frank McCourt, author of *Angela's Ashes*, said, "Good writers are very observant," he might have added that it's not enough for writers to notice the details around them; they must depict them for their audiences as well. And author Barry Lane, in his aptly titled book *After the End: Teaching and Learning Creative Revision*, points out that young writers who are too quick to the finish line can benefit from peer questions that extract rich detail and important information that readers crave. The point both of these authors are making is clear: as you make your way to The End, pay attention to that potential reader peering over your shoulder.

WHAT YOU NEED TO KNOW

- Contrary to what some might like to believe, we don't become good writers by reading a lot. Reading is passive, so while we appreciate vivid detail, we don't naturally acquire the skills necessary to produce it. It's

like appreciating a gourmet meal without having a clue how to cook; it only comes with good instruction and lots of practice.
- Youngsters *do* notice things, of course, and they recount experiences orally in colorful detail. They emit a storm of verbs, adverbs, and adjectives through facial expression, hand gesture, and voice inflection; in other words, they just need to trust themselves and write more like they talk.
- If the main objective of Moment One was to introduce students to the idea that their emotions are the drivers of inspiration, the goal of Revising Moment One is to get them to dig a little deeper for detail with help from their peers. While structure and mechanics are secondary, students should conclude their memoirs with a reflective paragraph, a skill they'll need to demonstrate as the year progresses.
- The questioning technique you will use here, Questions in the Margins (QIM), was developed by this author. Its purpose is to help developing writers retrieve details—those derived from the five senses, as well as thoughts and emotions—that are absent from their writing but alive and well in their memories. Their heads are full of details about that time they felt a strong emotion; they don't need to make anything up—just describe what's already there.
- QIM is most useful when applied to creative writing, so early training in peer-to-peer questioning will pay off as your students engage in personal-choice writing.

WHAT YOU NEED TO DO

- Set aside four periods for this process, but consider a fifth.
- Turn to textbox 2.1 and read an example of the QIM process before you go any further.

Textbox 2.1. An Example of the QIM Process

What follows is the beginning of a Moment One, written by a fictitious student, Manuel. The emotion that inspired this Moment One might have been sadness, for it's about losing a friend. Here's his first paragraph:

> Freddie was my friend. He lived next door to me, and we did stuff together all the time after school. It was a bad time for him back then, because his dad left the family and his mom had to get two jobs. Freddie and I even took care of his little brother sometimes after school, but on Saturdays my mom took care of him all day while Freddie's mom worked, so that was fun for us! But then they all moved to California because his mom and dad decided to get back together. That was two

years ago, and I really miss him. My mom and dad say that Freddie might come back and visit some day, and I hope he does. It's kind of lonely around here without him.

Now, let's say Manuel's teacher pairs him with a peer so he can get some Questions in the Margins before he goes any further. As his classmate reads the paragraph, she wonders about a few things and comes up with six mental questions: The first one ("What did Freddie look like?") comes to her when she reads the first sentence, so she writes it *in the margin* of Manuel's paper—right next to that sentence—and labels it Q1 for Manuel's benefit. The second sentence makes her wonder some more, so she writes Q2 under her first question and poses her second one: "What 'stuff' did you do together?"

The rest of her wonderings are recorded similarly: "What did you think about Freddie's dad?" "Why was Saturday so fun?" "How do you feel about Freddie now?" (In the meantime, Manuel is observing the process and thinking about how he's going to answer these queries and fit them into his paragraph.)

When his partner is finished noting her questions, Manuel returns to where his writing left off, *skips two lines*, and begins writing answers to his classmate's QIMs. He may write complete sentences or not—whatever he feels will work for him when he's adding this new information to his Moment One. He also needs to label these *answers* with the numbers that correspond to the questions: Q1, Q2, etc. Here's what Manuel wrote:

> Q1 Freddie was a lot smaller than me, but everything else was big. He had a round head, with black hair hanging over his ears, big brown eyes, and his smile was big too.
>
> Q2 We had fun practicing soccer kicks in the park across from us. Sometimes other kids would join in and we would have a match. One time we built a tree house in the park too, but some workmen came and took it down after a while.
>
> Q3 Sometimes Freddie's dad was okay, even kind of fun. But I think Freddie was afraid of him when he yelled at his mom.
>
> Q4 My mom took care of Marco, so Freddie and I had the whole day. Sometimes we played in the park, but sometimes we just laid in the grass and talked about stuff.
>
> Q5 I really liked Freddie, and I miss him because he was my best friend. I hope he's happy.

Then he marks the exact spots in his morphing Moment One memoir where he wants to insert his answers to Questions 1–5:

Freddie was my friend. (Q1) He lived next door to me, and we did stuff together all the time after school. (Q2) It was a bad time for him back then, because his dad left the family and his mom had to get two jobs. (Q3) Freddie and I even took care of his little brother sometimes after school, but on Saturdays my mom took care of him all day while Freddie's mom worked, so that was fun for us! (Q4) But then they all moved to California because his mom and dad decided to get back together. That was two years ago, and I really miss him. My mom and dad say that Freddie might come back and visit some day, and I hope he does. It's kind of lonely around here without him. (Q5)

Now, here's what his first (now two) paragraphs might look like:

Freddie was my friend. He was a lot smaller than me, but everything else was big. He had a round head, with black hair hanging over his ears, big brown eyes, and his smile was big too. He lived next door to me, and we did stuff together all the time after school, like practicing soccer kicks in the park across from us. Sometimes other kids would join in and we would have a match. One time we built a tree house in the park too, but some workmen came and took it down after a while.

It was a bad time for Freddie back then, because his dad left the family and his mom had to get two jobs. Sometimes his dad was okay, even kind of fun. But I think Freddie was afraid of him when he yelled at his mom. Freddie and I even took care of his little brother, Marco, sometimes after school, but on Saturdays my mom took care of him all day while Freddie's mom worked, so that was fun for us! We had the whole day. Sometimes we played in the park, but sometimes we just sat in the grass and talked about stuff. But then they all moved to California because his mom and dad decided to get back together. That was two years ago, and I really miss him. My mom and dad say that Freddie might come back and visit some day, and I hope he does. It's kind of lonely around here without him. I really liked Freddie, and I miss him because he was my best friend. I hope he's happy.

Day 1

- Have students bring their Moment Ones to the share circle and tell them what QIM stands for. Explain that when writers fail to describe a scene or character adequately, they force their audiences to wonder and fill in the blanks. Tell them that QIMs are a way for them to alert their classmates to these "wonderings." They can then create answers to the questions and custom fit them to their text.
- Ask them to think about their favorite books or stories and share how the authors used vivid detail. A great way to bring this home is to tell an off-the-cuff, boring story about two friends who met at the park, hung out awhile, went to get some food, went to one of their houses to eat it, and

played video games until the other one had to go home. (They might laugh, but they'll get the point that a lack of detail causes readers to wonder *a lot*.)
- Now ask for a volunteer to help you demonstrate the process. Have your guinea pig start reading his Moment One and listen for a few places that would benefit from more detail. At that point, stop the reading, give your volunteer a pencil, ask him a QIM, but tell him not to answer it orally. Then ask him if he knows why you asked the question and what he wrote that made you think of it. When he finds that place, tell him to write a capital Q1 in the margin next to it and write your question there. Repeat this process by asking another question or two.
- Explain to the class that QIMs can either be asked *orally* and jotted down by the author, or *written* on the author's paper by a peer or teacher. But *answering* QIMs orally is a waste of time, for the answers are the writer's concern; he needs time to think, and he's not yet sure which questions he will even choose to answer.
- Invite student participation. But before you have a few of them read a portion of their work and receive QIMs, explain the importance of asking about things that will lead to more detail—yes/no answers are usually dead ends. Also, tell your class to listen for descriptions that grew from the five senses and point out how powerful they are. Advise them that who, what, when, where, why, and how questions produce good information, as well as those inquiring about characters' thoughts and feelings.
- Introduce the idea that "questions" sometimes come in the form of leading statements—for example, "I would like you to write more about your family," or "Tell me what your brother looked like." And that's fine.
- Explain that, as mentioned above, students will not use all of the QIMs offered them, so it's important to give them many to choose from.
- If there's time left, have your students return to their seats and get a few QIMs from a classmate or two. (But don't let them start writing their answers to them yet.)

Day 2

- Pair up your students (or monitor self-selected pairs) to ensure maximum benefit for both partners. (An option is to rotate partners for fresh perspectives.) Tell them they'll spend roughly *half* of the period collecting QIMs—from *beginning to end* of their documents—and the other half writing their responses; meanwhile, you can circulate and contribute your own QIMs. To emphasize the importance of pushing each other for more detail, read aloud some particularly incisive questions and resulting responses.

Note: Explain that *answers* to QIMs will not be revisited until they're writing the final draft of this project.

Day 3

- Give the class about twenty minutes to wrap up any unanswered QIMs. Next, tell them to decide where *in their text* they want to place the answers and mark those spots with a Q1, Q2, etc.
- Next, ask students to turn their attention to the person who was either present as their emotional moment played out, or who appeared shortly thereafter. By now you will have driven home the importance of detail, so it will be a fun exercise for them to create a "close-up," detailed description—facial expression, body language, etc.—of the person. Explain that, because that individual was there, he or she must have had some sort of reaction to the situation—even an attitude of indifference would be interesting. (You might even ask students to write what they were thinking as they observed the person or speculate as to what the person was thinking as he stood by.)
- Allow the rest of this period for writing the close-up, and then have everyone identify and label the place where it will appear in his or her final—memoir—draft.

Day 4

- Address any concerns students might have about fitting QIM answers into their final drafts. Reassure them that their value lies in the information—the detail—and that how they incorporate it is up to them. They might have to add or delete words or sentences, but the important thing is to convey the added detail. (A demonstration from you would help.)
- Tell your class there is one more bit of writing to take care of, and that it will turn their Moment Ones into memoirs. Explain that a memoir is a reflection on a life lived, and that it includes lessons learned along the way. Ask your students to think about how their emotional experience affected them, how it changed them or caused them to look at things differently. Tell them that these thoughts should guide them as they write a paragraph to conclude their memoirs.

For instructional purposes, Manuel's memoir process focuses only on his opening paragraph, his close-up of Freddie, and his conclusion. The main body would have revealed more about the day that Freddie moved—the boys' conversations, interactions between parents, the sad good-bye, etc.—just as your students' memoirs will include lots of content from beginning to end.

Chapter Three

Student Biographies

This project might be better titled Biographical Essay. The final product is short, the research consists solely of one interview, and the format (introduction, body, and conclusion) is more like, well, an essay. There are two reasons this activity should be undertaken early in the year: (1) Classmates work in pairs to develop biographies of one another, and the process of interviewing and taking notes engages them in cooperative learning and facilitates socialization. (2) Students get to practice some skills—taking notes and organizing them into categories—that will be an important part of a more complex project offered in chapter 21, "Writing a Research Report."

WHAT YOU NEED TO KNOW

- Most of us probably think we're not important enough to be the subject of a biography, but children have the added burden of thinking they're not old enough. Your job is to convince them that their lives are unique and that they're worth writing and reading about. That said, it's true that older students are more experienced, so their biographies will run three or more typed pages, while first graders' life stories will probably require only one (or its printed equivalent).
- The density of these little biographies depends a lot on the diligence of the interviewer; for example, if a student asks his partner if she has any siblings, and she says yes, he should then ask about *each one*—his or her age, personality, education, job, role in the family, etc. It's amazing how many categories of information, and thus more paragraphs, can emerge from such an interview.
- Textbox 3.1 is a list of questions your biographers could ask each other, but you might want to add to it; the point is to keep them digging for more

and more information. A printable list of these questions is available on the *Keys to Inspiration* book page on Rowman & Littlefield's website. Notice that these queries are random, *not* categorized. This guarantees that students will have to do the work of organizing their notes into coherent topics that will form the body of the biography. (This is good practice for later projects.)

Textbox 3.1. Questions for Partners to Ask Each Other

What is your full name? Does it have a special meaning?
Where were you born?
What makes you happy?
Have you ever lived in another city? How was it different than this one?
Have you ever lived in another country? How did it differ from yours?
Have you lived in another neighborhood? How was it different than the one you're in now?
Have you ever moved to another school? What was that like?
How would you describe yourself?
Have you ever had a really interesting or unusual experience?
Have you ever done anything you wish you hadn't?
What makes you sad?
Have you traveled to other states or countries? Which ones, and why?
What types of books do you read? What's your favorite? Why?
Tell me about your parents.
Do they have jobs? What do they do?
Tell me about your siblings, or what it's like to be an only child.
Do you have relatives in another country?
What do you know about your heritage (your ancestors)?
Has anyone in your family ever been very sick or suffered a serious injury?
What makes you worry?
Do you have any pets? Tell me about them. Have you ever lost a pet?
Tell me about your grandparents and great-grandparents.
What was the most exciting thing you've ever done?
Do you have any hobbies? Tell me about them.
Are you involved in organized sports? Tell.
Do you take lessons (tennis, chess, swimming, dance)?
What was your all-time favorite school project or lesson?

What do you want to learn more about? Why?
How have you changed since you were in kindergarten?
What would you change about your life if you could?
What makes you angry?
Does your family celebrate special events or hold religious ceremonies? Which ones?
Whom do you look up to (admire) in your family? Why?
Do you have a hero or shero? Who? Why?
Why do you like your best friend?
What do you think you are really good at?
Are you proud to be you? Why or why not?
Do you think about what you might want to do when you grow up?
Tell me about the most emotional experiences you've had.
Have you learned any important lessons about life?
Have you been disappointed by anyone or anything so far in life?
What are your greatest hopes about the future?

WHAT YOU NEED TO DO

- A few weeks before you launch this project, set aside two half-periods for prebiography preparation and five full periods for interviewing, taking notes, organizing notes, and in-class writing.
- In the first (short) session, familiarize your class with the biography genre: Discuss why they're written and what they reveal about the subjects' lives. Explain the etymology of the word—it's from two Greek words: *bios*, which means "life," and *graphe*, which means "writing." Tell students that you'll be assigning them each a biographee in a few weeks and that they must read a biography or two before they begin the process themselves. If you're a primary teacher, you probably have several that you could read aloud. Older kids are likely to have read some at this point in their lives; if not, point them to the library.

Note: There's no need at this juncture to tell your students they'll be writing biographies about each other; it will only distract from the run-up and invite lobbying for favored partnerships.

- Conduct the other (short) session a few days before you begin the lesson. Ask students to share what they've learned about biographies, and see if they've picked up on some of the common topics they address: childhood, family life, education, jobs, life's hurdles, formative experiences, role models, contributions to society, etc. Then tell them to bring a pack of three-by-five note cards on the appointed day and meet their biographees, their fellow classmates!

Meanwhile, a bit of homework will prepare you to guide them through the note-taking process:

- Turn to figure 3.1, a sample note card for research projects.[1] You will not be duplicating it for this project—three-by-five cards will suffice—but you'll want your biographers to practice using *three* of its parts: "Note," "For What Reason?," and "Like or Unlike What?" (Explaining these parts on Day 1 will be easier if you download the card's image from the *Keys to Inspiration* book page on Rowman & Littlefield's website and project it while students follow along.)

Source _____ Page # _____ Student's Initials _____

1. SUBJECT (Use later in your sentences.)   **NOTE-TAKING CARD**

2. NOTE

3. FOR WHAT REASON?

4. LIKE OR UNLIKE WHAT?   5. AN EXAMPLE?
                                                       6. A DEFINITION?

TOPIC _____ SUBTOPIC _____
[LEVEL 3]

Figure 3.1. Sample note card for research projects. This note-taking card was developed by Thea Holtan.

- Notice a space labeled "Note." You'll be directing them to use the same relative space on their three-by-fives to record their interview notes. Insist that notes be kept short—no complete sentences—and that they'll be adding words later to create complete thoughts.
- Also locate "For What Reason?" and consider the following scenario: A student interviewer, Tom, finds out that his partner, Jared, has two broth-

ers, Jimmy and Johnny. During the interview, Jared mentions that Jimmy no longer lives at home, so Tom writes the note "brother gone" and continues pelting Jared with questions. At some point, Jared mentions that Jimmy is in the army, so Tom writes that down on a card and moves on. Later, he learns that Jimmy wanted Johnny to join the army with him, but he decided to stay at home and play in his band. So where does all of this lead?

- When the interviews are over, students will consider all of the other parts of their note cards, fill them in if appropriate, and use that information to formulate sentences. In Tom's case, he will have remembered *why* Jimmy didn't live at home, recorded that *reason*, and perhaps even filled in the "Like or Unlike What?" space on that card. His final biography will then likely contain the following sentences: "Jared's brother Jimmy doesn't live at home, *unlike* his brother Johnny. Jimmy wanted Johnny to join the army with him, but he decided to stay home and play in his band."

Note: It's important to understand that note cards are all different. Several will have *reasons* for notes, and one or two might have all six questions filled in, but the vast majority will only address one or two beyond the note itself. For this assignment, your students are only concerned with notes, reasons, and likes/unlikes, which will prepare them well for projects to come.

- Finally, pair up your students; avoid "friend" partnerships, and match up those who achieve at slightly different skill levels. (If you have an uneven number of students, simply create a group of three or—better yet—offer yourself as partner to the odd one out; you'll both love it!)

Day 1

- Launch the process. Start by explaining the note card. If you project it, students can see where to *pencil* in their initials and their subject (partner's name in this case). Also, have them write "Note," "Reason," and "Like/Unlike" in the appropriate spots. Give them time to label about 15 or 20 cards; they'll produce more as needed.
- Hand out *one* copy of the interview questions to each *pair* of students. Explain that they will only take notes this first day, and remind them not to enter them as complete sentences, just simply worded facts.
- Before you let them loose, demonstrate how to ask questions that lead to answers that lead to more questions and answers. Ask one of your students a question from the list: Q: Do you have a hero or shero? A: Yes. Q: Who? A: My dad. Q: Why him? A: He always listens to me. Q: What about your mom? A: She's really busy. Q: What does she do? A: She's not home a

lot. Q: Where does she go? A: She's a lawyer for a big company, so she travels all over the country. They'll get the idea.
- Tell your pairs to begin, and to take their time asking and answering questions. As they proceed, circulate to make sure the note cards have only notes on them and that they're asking follow-up questions. At the end of the period, collect the question sheets and have students put rubber binders around their cards and store them until tomorrow.

Day 2

- Finish *note taking* and move on to *reasons* and *likes/unlikes*. After students have produced at least 25 note cards, tell them to consider reasons for their notes. Again, use a student's note card to demonstrate. Then move on to likes and unlikes, also using a student's note as an example. But remember, students need to understand that many notes will not have reasons, and that even fewer will have likes or unlikes.

Day 3

- Organize notes. Tell students to take their top note card and place it in front of them. Next, have them look at the second card and decide if the note is related to the first one. If it is, it will go on top of it; if not, it will become the first card in a second pile. (This is the beginning of the process of determining topics for the body of the biography.) They should continue this process until they have three to five topics of *at least* two or three notes each. "Leftovers" should be given a chance to find a home, but sometimes they just need to be tossed out. Once finalized, the topic piles need to be bound or clipped to avoid mix-ups.
- Once this is finished, your students can think about names for their topic piles—for example, "family," "places lived," "parents' jobs," and "adjusting to schools"—and decide what *order* they should take in the biography.

Day 4

- Introductory and body paragraphs, general statements. At this point, teach them how to write an introduction. It must open by identifying the subject and then mention the topics, in order, without giving away any details; for example, "*Laura* has had an interesting and busy life so far. Her large *family* has *lived* in many cities around the country, because her *parents* have changed *jobs* many times. That means that she has had to *change schools*, too." Tell your students that these are called *general statements* because they don't give away *specifics*. (You might also take the opportu-

nity here to explain the connection between these terms and the words *genus* and *species*.)
- Next, tell your class to write their brief introductions and then begin their body paragraphs, reminding them that they must appear in the same order they took in their introductions. Urge them to take their time—to think about how they can create sentences from the information on their note cards—even weave together parts from two separate cards.

Note: Some of your students might know how to create *topic sentences*—even *transitional sentences*—but for this early-in-the-year project you might want to put these off for later lessons, where these elements are fully explained.

Day 5

- Day 5 is for finishing the biography, but first talk to your writers about conclusions. They represent what writers *conclude* as they reflect on what they've learned about a subject; it's the takeaway that's passed on to the reader. Remind them about the memoir project (chapter 2) and how they concluded it by revealing what they learned about themselves as a result of the Moment One experience. If your students understand this, they should be able to complete an acceptable concluding paragraph.

Note: "Proper" conclusions, those that we associate with essays, articles, or research reports, are difficult for kids, and yours will have ample opportunity to wrestle with the idiosyncrasies later on in this book. You should think about it now, though, because it's important to recognize that most conclusions are not exactly ends; in fact, one way or another, they usually finish with "an eye to the future"—again, similar to the memoir conclusions. Considering all of this, then, it would seem perfectly appropriate for your biographers to speculate about their subjects' futures.

- Devote the rest of the period to wrapping the assignment up.

Option

Create silhouettes of your class members and put them up in the hall next to their biographies. It makes for a wonderful display, and students enjoy identifying their peers and reading their life stories.

- You'll need a projector, a stool, twelve-by-eighteen-inch sheets of black construction paper, a couple of white oil-pastel crayons, a roll of masking tape, and a flat, out-of-the-way vertical surface, like a chalkboard.

- While your students are writing on the last two days of the project, have them come to you one at a time. Seat them on the stool, in profile, right in front of the chalkboard. Turn on the projector, hold a sheet of the paper against the board, and adjust it so that the individual's head, hair, and a bit of neck *almost* fill it up. Next, put a rolled-up piece of tape behind the top corners to hold it in place. (If this is done right, you should only have to make minor, if any, adjustments with each new student.)
- Begin by telling the subject not to move—at all! If his chin drops, tap it up. Order him to take slow, shallow breaths and stare straight ahead. (You might want to tape a piece of paper at eye level on a far wall to help with this.) Assure him that if he doesn't move he'll only have to endure this once.
- Now, just trace the silhouette; it's fast and easy, and it yields an amazingly sharp image. (When doing the hair, create suggestions of curls and waves and puffs and pigtails.) Once you get the hang of it, you can do most of a class in one period, with only two or three do-overs.

Note: It's nice to mix up the profile directions (right or left) so they can "look at each other" in the hall display.

NOTE

1. This note-taking card was developed by Thea Holtan for *Think, Organize, Write! The Thinking and Writing Process*, which is featured in chapter 21, "Writing a Research Report."

Chapter Four

Respect, the Booklet

R-E-S-P-E-C-T—Find out what it means to me.—Aretha Franklin

Like the Queen of Soul, we all know that respect is a good thing, but what does it really mean to us, and how do we show it? We talk about it a lot in school, but too often it's in reaction to a disrespectful act: Two students begin fighting in class, and learning stops. The teacher calls for help, forms are filed, and punitive steps are taken by administration. The next day there's a class discussion about the incident. The word *respect* comes up, but the two pugilists can't take part, for they've been suspended.

This project seeks to raise students' awareness of the myriad ways we manage to hurt each other, and the ripple effects that disrespectful actions bring to bear on communities. The idea is that mature, respectful behavior requires a shift in focus—away from oneself, and toward others. Teachers need to emphasize that hurtful behavior slows all of us down. It causes damage and replaces hope with fear. If one of society's goals is to make life better for all of us, then we must go forward together, respectfully.

WHAT YOU NEED TO KNOW

- Like all teachers, you have to deal with bad behavior, and you've noticed that some students have a stronger grip on concepts like *right and wrong*, *empathy*, and *personal responsibility* than others. Child development experts have noticed it too, and they've concluded that the path to mental maturity is not dictated by age, nor is it linear. It's as strongly influenced by social factors as it is by a person's stage in life, so it sometimes moves "sideways." But all parties agree that the road is a bumpy one for kids to navigate, and the best you can do is help smooth it out a bit.

- Young people naturally have a myopic view of themselves, but you can open their eyes to the bigger picture. This lesson gives kids a chance to discuss what it means to be respectful, consider the ramifications of less-than-acceptable behavior, and then create a booklet of artistic and written interpretations of such experiences.
- Negative behaviors are the focus here precisely because they're *not* the norm. When someone treats us *fairly*, we take it for granted—it's expected. Conversely, disrespectful actions can have long-lasting, even devastating, effects. So if students ask to share examples of respectful actions, indulge them; it serves to highlight the contrast between the two. The goal here is to provide youngsters the opportunity to look inward, assess their own behavior, and ponder their position on the maturity scale.

WHAT YOU NEED TO DO

- Set aside three periods, but be open to a fourth.
- Download the Respect Book page template (see figure 4.1) from the *Keys to Inspiration* book page on Rowman & Littlefield's website..
- Decide how many scenarios your students can handle (4, 8, 12, or 16 should cover all grade levels). Then divide that number by four and multiply the quotient by the number of students you have. Next, copy that

Respect Book Template

Who and/or What? _____   Who and/or What? _____
How? _____   How? _____

Ripples _____   Ripples _____

Figure 4.1. Respect Book template

many—*double-sided*—copies of the template. (Yes, four scenarios fit on one sheet, but a short booklet might be just fine for first graders.)
- Obtain nine-by-twelve-inch construction paper (for booklet covers) and decide which colors would be best suited for student illustrations, titles, etc. Next, place *two* blank eight-and-a-half-by-eleven sheets of paper under *a set* of template sheets and fold them all neatly in half. Then fold the cover sheet in half and staple the two parts together along the fold. Voilà! A booklet. The bottom blank sheet (fly leaf) will remain blank, but the other one will be a *title page* on the first side, a *copyright page* on the second side, and an *about the author* paragraph on the third side, which appears in the back of the booklet. (The fourth side of that sheet can remain blank.) Staple the rest of the booklets.
- Review the examples (at the end of this chapter) of disrespectful acts, the places they occur, the people or things that suffer as a result, and the effects they have on others. Have these, as well as ones that you want to add, on hand as you introduce the project.

Day 1

- Gather in the share circle and tell your students they're about to have a conversation about respect and disrespect in preparation for a small writing and art project. Start out by asking what these two terms mean, but don't expect precise definitions. Instead, you will hear many examples of "good" and "bad" behaviors, but that's okay; the point here is to discuss a broad range of disrespectful acts—from butting in line to online bullying.
- Continue by asking them about times when they felt disrespected, observed others being disrespected, or acted disrespectfully themselves. (Some students will want to contribute examples of behavior that they witnessed but were not a party to. That's fine, but warn them not to identify people other than themselves.)
- Turn it up a notch: Explain how one disrespectful act can cause a *ripple effect*—a chain of *re*-actions that radiate out, affecting people beyond the initial victim. Some fade away or get resolved, but others last a long time. (This might be an opportunity to talk about how hard it is to "put the genie back in the bottle.")
- Introduce the idea that *things*, as well people, can be disrespected—rights, rules, authority, property—and invite students to share examples of those instances too.
- Explain that they'll be making a simple little booklet featuring illustrations of disrespectful behavior, as well as written explanations of who or what was being disrespected, how the scenario played out, and who else was affected.

Note: This first day is intense. It will be a cathartic experience for more than a few, so be prepared to extend the discussion into Day 2. (In either case, it's time to tell your students how many examples of behaviors and consequences they'll be representing in their books.)

Day 2

- Continue the first day's discussion or move on to explain examples of what your students will be writing and drawing.
- Show your class a blank booklet so they can envision how their content will fit the format.
- Transcribe to your board, or project, the following examples of what a student might write at the bottom of a page:

    1. Who and/or What? Our school's *property* was disrespected. How? Someone sprayed gang graffiti all over the fence around the playground. Ripples? It scared us, and the playground was closed a long time while it was being scrubbed off.
    2. Who and/or What? My self-esteem was disrespected. How? A boy in my class put a picture of me on Facebook and said I was fat. It hurt. Ripples? I'm embarrassed to go to school now.

- Explain that these statements need to be concise, neat, and written in pencil to allow for correction of mistakes.
- As for artwork, be open: Some students will create realistic images of people, while others might employ stick figures. For the playground example above, the artist might not depict people at all—perhaps just an empty field surrounded by a graffiti-covered fence.
- If time allows, let students begin their work. Then circulate, checking for mechanical errors and neatness; it's quick, for there's not a lot of text. Use a light pencil, tell them to fix all of the mistakes, and remind them that books don't contain mechanical errors!

Day 3 (or 4)

- Continue to proofread students' work as they finish up the project, assign a due date for those who don't finish, and plan to have students read their booklets aloud.

Options

- While it's presumptuous to assume that older students are less likely than their younger counterparts to enjoy and appreciate the opportunity to illustrate their thoughts, they might prefer to write an essay instead. If you offer them that option, make sure they follow the essay guidelines in this book. You will also have to help them organize *three categories* of disrespectful behaviors to be addressed in the essay's body paragraphs, and go over the tricky task of formulating *general statements*.
- Make a respect poster: In tall capital letters, print R-E-S-P-E-C-T, including the hyphens. Then print the following words, *vertically*, under their respective (no pun intended) initial letters: Rules Everyone Should Practice, Else Chaos Triumphs.

In preparation for your discussions surrounding respect and its antonym, consider the following categories:

1. People—We often disrespect those closest to us (*ourselves*, parents, siblings, grandparents), but others are not immune (friends, school staff, classmates, bus drivers, neighbors, even strangers).
2. Things—authority, laws, rules, rights, property, and privacy; others' opinions, time, and trust; privileges, responsibilities, commitments, and promises; others' health, safety, security, and personal space; others' age, body shape, weight, dress, and sexual identity; and others' religion, culture, skin color, ethnicity, native language, and social status.
3. Disrespectful acts—betrayal, dishonesty, disloyalty, bullying, serious teasing, stealing, vandalism, name-calling, gossiping, pushing, interrupting, disrupting, physical assault, verbal assault, harassment, and inappropriate touch.
4. Places—home, school, public transit, neighborhoods, stores, parks, and playgrounds.
5. Ripple effects for those who are disrespected—fear, anger, hate, distrust, vindictiveness, hopelessness, anxiety, loss of energy, injury, physical and emotional scars, low self-esteem, stomach aches, eating disorders, insomnia, social withdrawal and isolation, and dealing with the thought that your family might have to move to escape the problem.
6. Ripple effects for those who are disrespectful—loss of privileges and being grounded, being suspended or expelled from school, losing the respect of others, and facing the difficult process of accepting blame and correcting behavior.

7. Ripple effects for those related to an offending individual—having to meet with school officials or police, having to drive a student to school because he was banned from the bus, struggling with how to address the bad behavior of someone close.

Chapter Five

Writers' Workshop

This model of classroom management works, but it must be flexible. Early proponents of the system called on teachers to keep a running record of *each* student's progress in *all* areas of writing, including mechanics—right down to the last punctuation mark! This plan must have cost language arts teachers oodles of time, especially those secondary English instructors who were charged with teaching both literature *and* writing to as many as 180 students a day.

The structure of a Writers' Workshop makes sense—a short mini-lesson, writing time, and a share session—but there's a problem: Writing is a complex subject. When school leaders and curriculum gurus dictate schedules and content, they assume that teachers will be able to squeeze every child into the same-size outfit. They can try, but they'll need to take some liberties with the prescribed daily routine.

Note: Teachers who are working with 90-minute blocks need to split that time equally between reading and writing—flexibility *within* Writers' Workshop doesn't imply that it's acceptable to let reading activities encroach on writing time.

Mini-lessons are for explaining things (mechanics rules, paper-airplane folding, an upcoming field trip), but they can also be hijacked by a teacher who must deal with an emergent issue. It's like triage in the ER . . . an epidemic of bad grammar is spreading throughout the school. She hears students and teachers alike say, "I should have *went*," and "I could have *ran*," and yells, "Quick! Someone hand me the irregular-verb chart!"

In a 175-day school year, you'll find it difficult to find time to cover all of the content and mechanics rules that govern writing, let alone the occasional instructions and explanations; furthermore, big or messy projects will crowd out a few mini-lessons altogether. So your job is to identify the *most common problems* that are holding your students back, and then decide which ones are important enough to address as a whole class. (A healthy Writers' Workshop will naturally encourage peers to help each other with content and mechanics issues as well.)

Writing time is sacrosanct—everyone in the business agrees that our children aren't writing enough, and that they can't get better without lots of practice—but it too must be flexible. Sometimes a mini-lesson eats into it, or you decide to allow more students to read their work during a share session. Again, you can't do everything. The good news is that if you manage to get your kids hooked, they'll be more engaged during the time they have in class, and they'll work harder to improve their writing; what's more, they'll spend more time writing at home, which is something that many young writers actually *prefer*.

Writers like to be comfortable, but—let's face it—most classrooms aren't. Make the best of it by providing floor pillows and an upholstered chair or two. The lighting should be low, and tables are better than desks. Some write to music and others can't stand it; be judicious. Ask for silence, but settle for on-task whispering. Finally, don't hover over their shoulders; they'll let you know when it's safe to ask some questions.

Writers can be very random, and the more they observe and feel life, the more they want to write about it. Let them experiment and abandon pieces they lose interest in. Writing time is for making progress on assignments, yes, but it's also a time for students to find their inner writer and learn who they are. Remember, too, that your students should be keeping up with their Open Topic writing (explained in the introduction), so that is always an option during this portion of Writers' Workshop.

Holding teacher–student conferences during writing time is part of the Writers' Workshop routine. Its purported purpose is to get a handle on each student's progress, presumably to update the teacher records referred to in the first paragraph of this chapter. Some question the efficacy of the practice, however, and wonder if a student conferee would be better off spending his time writing, while his teacher spent hers offering constructive feedback to his fellow classmates. It's up to you to decide how best to apply your talents.

The *share session* might better be called the *share circle*, that ancient symbol of inclusivity. When your students come together in a circle to talk about their writing, all pretenses evaporate. There's no hierarchy; you are there as a moderator, not the authority. No one's back is turned, and constructive criticism is the rule—it's a wonderful thing to witness.

To begin, ask for volunteers to read their works in progress, remembering that there will be time for only a few; as a result, those who perpetually offer to step forward will have to be restrained, and those who shy away from going public should be nudged from time to time, but not pushed; they're still benefiting from the discussions. (Advise your readers to take notes as their classmates provide feedback.)

Next, remind students what to listen for. Good content contains *details* that paint a clear picture of people, places, things, action, and thoughts; it avoids repetition of words and phrases; and it doesn't leave readers confused about the order of events. These are the things that young writers must get right and that their colleagues can help them with.

After a reading, call for comments and questions from the group. Ask them what they were *wondering* as their fellow student read her piece. Explain that these "wonderings" often indicate something's missing, and thereby alert the author that she might need to revise her work.

Also, tell them to avoid questions that can be answered with a quick yes or no. These are dead-end queries that elicit little if any useful information. Better to ask who, what, when, where, and why, or questions about what something looked like, sounded like, smelled like, tasted like, or felt like (emotionally or texturally). Or how about, "What was that character *thinking* when he . . . ?" (*Implied* questions are also helpful for the author; for example, "Partway through your reading, I got lost; I didn't know which character you were talking about.")

Note: It would be appropriate here to use the questioning technique described in chapter 2, "Revising Moment One."

There's an unspoken sense of community in a Writers' Workshop classroom, and its presence is especially felt during the share session. This little meeting, where students offer each other truly constructive criticism, is a confidence builder and driver of student progress. Interestingly, it's comparable to adult writing groups that come together for support and advice, many of whose members are struggling with the same insecurities and skill issues as their young counterparts. Sharing ideas about writing, whether we're old or young, spurs us on to write more, and that's a good thing.

Finally, consider setting up an "editorial roundtable." As your year progresses, you'll be able to let several students at a time gather at a special place set up for group editing. It's very effective, for you can choose writers of all skill levels to join. No one stands out as an "expert" or "failure," for student work is passed around the table—everyone offers editing and proofreading advice to everyone else, but there are rules, of course. Each editor has to be positive that a proofreader's mark is necessary and appropriate. Spelling mistakes must be real mistakes—not "maybes"—before a word is circled to indicate a misspelling, for example. And speaking of spelling, a student checking for errors needs to start at the *end* of the sample being worked on. He should then read backward, word by word, to avoid "reading ahead" and missing mistakes.

Outfit the table with a list of rules, a copy of the proofreader's marks sheet referred to in chapter 6, several sharpened pencils, some fine-point pastel markers, and an eraser or two. You'll be heartened to see how this cooperative arrangement improves students' mechanical skills and exposes them to their classmates' abilities. You might even call it a mentoring table.

Chapter Six

Assessment

While the Common Core (and myriad other) writing standards seem harmless enough, today's common teacher corps seems to struggle with their implementation. One problem is that standards are just goals; developing curricula to meet them is another matter, and that job is left to school districts, individual schools, or teachers. Naturally, this results in programs that are all over the map. The other problem is that, despite the call for more student-centered instruction, the standards spawn curricula that remain largely "top down." Achievement in writing depends on emotional investment from the bottom, that is, the students. Without it, the standards, as well as the writing lessons that purport to address them, make little sense.

The role of the writing teacher, then, is to understand exactly what qualifies as good writing, pass that knowledge on to students, and manage time to allow for maximum output from student writers and meaningful assessment—a tall order; in short, he or she has to be realistic and focus on the important stuff.

WHAT YOU NEED TO KNOW

- The more your students write, the less you'll have to assess. What? Yes, students get quite a bit better just by practicing. As for the kids who can't seem to get started, it's a matter of trusting their emotions, committing them to paper, and getting that initial, positive feedback that will motivate them to write more.
- Even very young writers should be producing more than you can read, much less assess. Think about a high school teacher who has 160 students: how much writing could she allow each student to produce—every day or

- even every week—if she planned to read and evaluate their collective work? And if she teaches reading and literature too?
- Abandoning a piece of writing is okay, especially free writing, or what's referred to as Open Topic writing in this book; if they're writing *anything*, they're practicing skills and pursuing their writer's truth. Specific assignments are another matter, however. They need to finish them, which is why they have to be emotionally connected to them.
- Teacher feedback is crucial. Once kids are emotionally inspired, you can assume they care about their writing; therefore, they care about your comments and corrections. Ask some Questions in the Margins (QIMs); compliment them on word choice; and tell them their content is impressive—writers can smell genuine input, and it spurs them on.

WHAT YOU NEED TO DO

- If you're an elementary teacher, remember: don't let the reading portion of your language arts block spill over into writing time. If you're a secondary teacher, carve out as much time as you can for writing—perhaps a period or two per week. If you're a writing specialist, your students are very lucky!
- Search online for Six+1 Trait Writing and register to download a free description of the seven traits. This rubric is a concise, handy reference, and it identifies the skills that writers need to acquire as they progress toward mastery (Content/Ideas, Conventions, Organization, Sentence Fluency, Word Choice, Voice, and Presentation). Post it in your classroom, explain it thoroughly, and let your students know you'll be using it to assess their work.

Note: Those of you who still provide handwritten feedback on student papers might want to check out the rubber stamp that's illustrated in figure 6.1.[1] Its initials represent the seven traits, and the lines next to them can be used to assign points. These points could align with a teacher-devised scale or reflect values suggested by the Six+1 Trait folks (Beginning, 1; Emerging, 2; Developing, 3; Capable, 4; Experienced, 5; Exceptional, 6). While these numbers do not reveal how students are doing in the *subcategories* of the traits—*Conventions* includes grammar, punctuation, and spelling, for example—they let students know where they need to improve, and they help teachers calculate grades. Also, understand that you don't always have to record a value for *every* trait; you might want to reserve that option for "heavily weighted" assignments.

- Check out the sample markup in figure 6.2, which demonstrates how teachers can give feedback on content and mechanics, as well as pose QIMs. It could be a quick snapshot at any stage of a student's effort, or a longer look before making a final assessment, in which case the Six+1 Trait stamp would probably be added. (Notice the teacher's initials below the line, indicating where he stopped commenting.)
- You'll also want to familiarize yourself with the proofreader's marks in figure 6.3. Most of them are conventional; a few were invented by the author.
- Decide which writing lessons and projects you're going to assess thoroughly and factor into your students' progress reports, but don't tell them which ones they'll be. This keeps them on their toes, especially if you let them know you're going to record grades for some of the shorter assignments too. (It also sends the message that everything they write is important.)

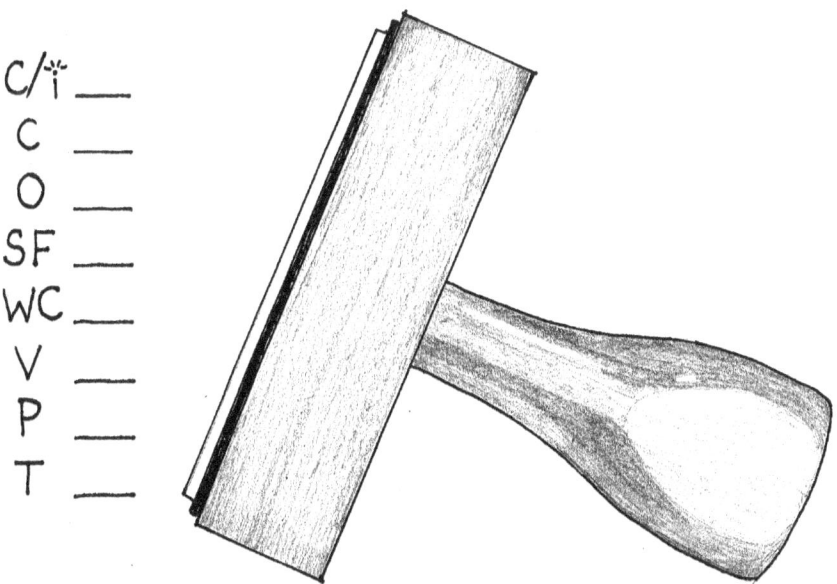

Figure 6.1. Rubber stamp. Art by Elizabeth Ford.

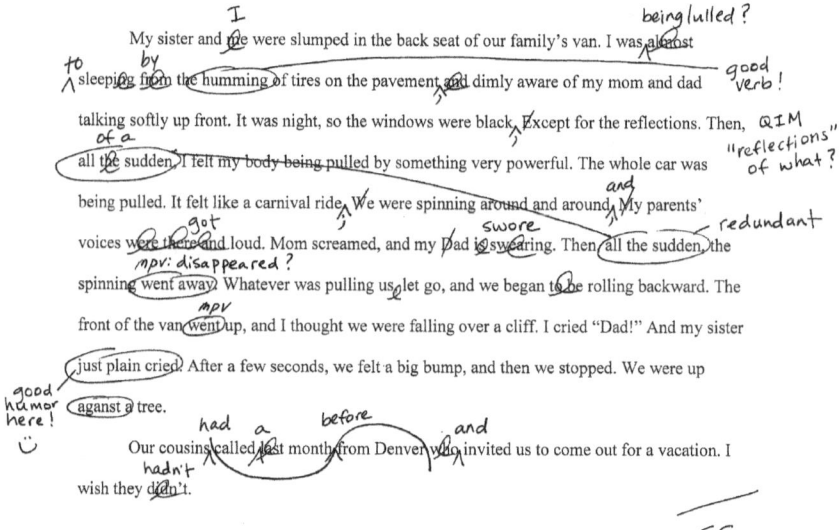

Figure 6.2. Sample markup

Note: You'll spend more time assessing the formally graded projects, but give all assignments a once-over for your students' benefit.

- Do yourself and your students a favor—incorporate some assessment into the Writers' Workshop. During writing time, circulate around the room, armed with a clipboard, and jot down notes regarding your writers' progress. While you're at it, offer a QIM here or correct a grammar mistake there. You're a mobile troubleshooter, zeroing in on problems—in real time—and moving on. These "mini-conferences" are more beneficial for teachers *and* students than scheduled, longer meetings that pull students from their work; they build confidence and keep pencils moving.

Note: "Grading on the fly" is especially efficient for monitoring progress on multicomponent assignments, such as the research project featured in chapter 21. Students simply lay out their note cards, outlines, etc., and you come by and check them off.

- Finally, feel good about the work you're doing. Teaching and assessing writing is not easy, and when our education system seems to be conflicted about its importance, you might wonder why you should care so much, but *do*. Hopefully, the exercises and projects presented in the following chapters will take hold, and your students will write volumes—more than you even have time to read.

Assessment

Proofreader's Marks

Mark	Meaning	Mark	Meaning
ℓ	Delete	#	Insert space
⊙	Add a period	⌒	Close space
≡	Capitalize	mpv	More powerful verb here
/	Make lower case	¶	Make a new paragraph
⌒	Misspelled word	inc.	Incomplete sentence
⌒sp	Spell out	awk.	Awkward wording
∧	Insert (something) here	w.c.	Poor word choice
∨ ∨	Insert apostrophe or single quotation mark	t.	Wrong tense
∧	Insert comma	ital.	Set in italics
∨ ∨	Insert quotation marks	⊓	Move up
;|	Insert semicolon	⊔	Move down
:|	Insert colon	stet	Let it stand
=	Insert hyphen	?	Insert question mark
∽	Transpose (short)	M	Insert em dash
Transpose (long) she (loudly sang)		Redundant nice — nice nice	

Figure 6.3.

NOTE

1. Yes, they still do make rubber stamps! Just find a company online and describe the one pictured in figure 6.1. It will cost about fifteen dollars, but it's worth it.

Chapter Seven

Commonalities

General to Specific

If we expect young writers to master most every type of written expression by the time they finish high school, it makes sense to teach them not only the components that define each type of writing but also how and where those components turn up in other forms. Armed with this information, students will create mental templates that give them a bird's-eye view and guide them as they take on a variety of projects. Some of these commonalities are general and speak to the broad spectrum of written expression, while others are more specific—zeroing in on structure and the more subtle issue of word choice. If students can identify and internalize them, they'll have an easier time navigating their way through projects of increasing complexity.

General commonalities are closely related, and they sum up the writing process quite neatly: *emotion inspires* us to write, our *thoughts* hijack our pencils, and together we create a *beginning*, *middle*, and *end*.

WHAT YOU NEED TO KNOW

- *Emotion* and *inspiration* are nearly synonymous, and when they are brought together and recorded, we call it writing. This common trait should drive your curriculum.
- *Thinking*. While emotion is a potent catalyst for writing, it can only come to fruition if we let our *thoughts* take hold of our pencils and guide us. At that point, we aren't thinking of something to write; we're writing what we're thinking. One could say that thinking is writing that has yet to be recorded.

- *Beginning > Middle > End*—the mother of all manifestations of the passage of time—is the most obvious commonality, but it's more a fact of life than something to be taught. Its application to the various forms of writing, however, is something students need to learn.
- *An eye to the future* is the writer's invitation to look beyond the end. It can be stated directly or whispered softly into the reader's ear.
- *So what?* This is a term that author Nancie Atwell, Writers' Workshop guru, has suggested teachers invoke when assessing student work. It's a great question, for it weighs the impact of a piece of writing, and in that sense it begs another question: Is there *an eye to the future*?

Specific Commonalities

General Statements

- These appear in introductory paragraphs, where writers alert their readers to the specific topics that will follow, but do not reveal any facts.
- Similarly, they function as *topic sentences* in the body of the work; they indicate the *main idea* of each paragraph—again, without giving away any details that will follow.
- General statements are also found in *concluding paragraphs*, where writers, instead of rehashing "evidence" that was contained in the body, simply summarize it in an effort to secure the reader's favor.
- *Transitional sentences*, also a type of general statement, are sometimes used to end one paragraph by pointing readers to the next. They do not contain facts but merely foreshadow the main idea of the paragraph ahead.

Thesis Statements, Hypotheses, and Calls to Action

- The introduction to an essay includes a *thesis statement*, which represents its main idea; in the case of a *persuasive essay*, it's an opinion with which the writer hopes the reader will agree. In research, it's more like a *hypothesis* that the writer hopes to verify through investigation, and in an editorial it takes the form of a *call to action*—a solution to the problem that the writer exposed and analyzed.

Simile, Metaphor, Adjectives, Adverbs, and Powerful Verbs

- Simile and metaphor add meaning and detail through comparison, and at times they're so subtly stitched into the fabric of a narrative that we hardly notice. Consider the lovely simile in this passage from Mary Norton's *The Borrowers*: "Mrs. May taught her many things besides crochet: how to run-and-fell and plan a darn; how to tidy a drawer and to lay, *like a*

blessing, above the contents, a sheet of rustling tissue against the dust." Whereas similes use *like* or *as* to clarify or enhance meaning, metaphors skip those terms and simply give a name to something in order to make the comparison: "The giant oak in our backyard *was a mansion* occupied by the neighborhood critters." (The tree was not *like* a mansion; it *was* a mansion.)
- Adjectives, often considered the most important part of a sentence for their descriptive power, are very handy but hardly worthy of such praise; that title belongs to the verb. When they're paired with adverbs, however, which can "add" meaning to a verb or adjective, they form the core of *general statements*; for example, a topic sentence that reads, "The dams that beavers build are *very difficult* to maintain," tells the reader that the topic is all about building dams, but it reveals no facts about the actual process.
- General statements of all types lean heavily on *adjectives* and *adverbs*, for they help writers avoid the temptation to include details where they don't belong.

Note: Many of these commonalities have been described here in terms of how they apply to various projects contained in this book, but they are, in fact, universal. In that regard, make an effort to point them out to your students as you involve them in other writing projects.

WHAT YOU NEED TO DO

- Teach your students the vocabulary of general commonalities and be sure to dust them off and use them as you teach the various forms of writing.

    1. *Emotion* . . . (There is a list of emotions and emotion-related words in appendix C; you might want to copy several onto a poster for display.)
    2. *Thinking* . . . opining, ruminating, considering, pondering, wondering, questioning, comparing, contrasting, analyzing, evaluating, synthesizing
    3. *Beginning* . . . introduction, subject, thesis, hypothesis, preview, setting, characters
    4. *Middle* . . . guts, body, topics, details, evidence, substance, arguments, facts, opinions, problems, conflict
    5. *End* . . . summarization, reflection, hindsight, conclusion, review, result, lessons, change, takeaway, resolution, solution, answer, moral, point, proposal, reckoning, reconsideration

6. *So what?* . . . value, relevance, contribution, information, wisdom, direction, inspiration, truth
7. *An eye to the future* . . . survival, rebirth, reward, renewal, resilience, hope

FINAL NOTE

Consider the idea that concepts like *beginning > middle > end* and *an eye to the future* appear almost everywhere . . .

1. In the modest haiku:

    eagle eyes his prey
    diving, talons sinking in
    he hauls it aloft

2. Even in a recipe:

    Gather ingredients . . .
    Prepare . . .
    Serve . . .
    Enjoy . . .

Chapter Eight

Dramatic Details

If almost all writing is inspired to some degree by emotion, and if language arts teachers expect their students to infuse characters with genuine feelings, then they might do well to borrow a page from their colleagues in the drama department; playwrights and directors teach an actor how to "become" a character—to adopt its voice, movement, and facial expressions—not just recite monotonous lines. The task of a writer is similar, but arguably harder.

While an actor moves through a play carrying a bundle of character traits that he can demonstrate at will, a writer must record a *description* of voice, body language, or facial expression each time a character appears; furthermore, he has to avoid using redundant language! Yes, writing is hard, but students can learn to use words to bring their characters alive, just as actors use their bodies.

WHAT YOU NEED TO KNOW

- Theater directors implore their actors to "say it with feeling." The reason is obvious, of course, but student writers need to understand how it applies to them, for emotion plays as crucial a role in writing as it does in acting. Writers and actors both deal in body language, voice, and movement, but live actors, unlike fixed words on a novelist's page, are flexible. Directors can fine-tune their physical and emotional expression to nudge them closer to the playwright's vision. Novelists and other writers get one shot at creating mood and movement; their words are permanent—inflexible—so they can only hope their readers interpret them as they intended.
- This activity is not about acting; it's about creating looks. Students of writing need to study the infinite ways that living creatures physically arrange themselves when conveying emotion. It's similar to the world of

music—before a musician can play a tune, she must learn and internalize the rudiments.
- These exercises should occupy only 15 or 20 minutes, and they should be spread out over several weeks. Students will need time to digest them—to think about how they can communicate emotion by detailing what it "looks like."

WHAT YOU NEED TO DO

Following are several iterations of this activity. As you present each of them, it's important to call on your students to imagine—out loud—how they would form written descriptions of the expressions demonstrated by their peers.

Homework

- Study the emotion-related lists in appendix C ("Emotions and Emotion-Related Words," "Facial Expressions," and "Facial Features, Hands"), keeping in mind that the first lesson will involve *only* facial expressions. You'll need to cull out only a few, for it's better to have several students take a crack at the *same* emotion until all are comfortable with the process.

Note: Take a look at the "Moral/Ethical Vocabulary" list too; you might get some ideas for activities to follow.

Activity 1

- Remind your class that emotion exists in almost all forms of writing, and that expressing it requires just as much attention to detail as describing colors or shapes or sizes. The difference is that emotion is not tangible; we can't refer to it as *red* or *square* or *big*. We have to find words—beyond *happy* and *sad* and *angry*—to reveal a character's mood; in fact, we should be able to capture a person's mood without using those tired terms at all!
- Emphasize the importance of choosing alternatives to hackneyed words and phrases when depicting emotion: "Anna smiled" or "Anna's happy" does the job, but "As Anna opened the present, her eyes brightened and her cheeks crinkled, revealing deep dimples" works too. We know when we read, "Andy had an angry look on his face" that he's angry, but "As Andy stared into the man's eyes, he raised his upper lip, revealing clenched teeth" is better.

- Finally, arrange your students in a circle (the preferred orientation for all of these sessions). Ask for a volunteer to project an emotion from your list—something simple, like "happy"—using only his face. After the demonstration, ask the group to identify what convinced them that the expression was happiness—eyes? eyebrows? mouth? Then invite them to tell how they would describe their peer's expression if they were to write about it.

Activity 2

- Now that your students have had a chance to use the *entire* face to express emotion, start limiting them to combinations of facial features (eyes and mouth; lips, teeth, and jaw; etc.). Stick with easy-to-project emotions, however; restricting their features will be challenge enough. Give them a chance to try conveying emotions using only the eyes; they are the most versatile vehicle of expression there is. (You might, in fact, want to devote a few sessions to the face, for this reason alone.)

Activity 3

- Introduce your budding thespians to some words that define *attitudes*. While they're not—strictly speaking—emotions, they come close, and they help writers by suggesting emotions that might be underlying them. Make up a list of your own: *skepticism, disbelief, bemusement, defiance, impatience, indifference, confidence, boredom, disgust, disappointment, calm, suspicion,* or *doubt*. Notice that these nouns can also be expressed as adjectives and that adjectives can also describe attitudes: *dismissive, aloof, uppity,* or *distracted,* for example. Then have your students try communicating these attitudes through facial expression.

Activity 4

- From strictly facial demonstrations of attitude, segue into standing poses that combine facial expression and positioning of arms, legs, feet, and torso. Students will feel liberated if they can portray *defiance*, for example, by crossing their arms, leaning back a bit, and shaking their head back and forth ever so slightly.

Activity 5

- Free their bodies through verbs and adverbs! You start it off by moving through the middle of the circle, saying, "The teacher *tip-toed silently* across the room and out the door." Then order your class to spread out randomly; pick a student and say, "John *slalomed gracefully* through the crowd and *slipped* out of the room." Reestablish the circle and try another: "Lucy *sank slowly* to her knees, *crept* under the table, and fell asleep." Decide if you want to let students come up with some of these verb–adverb combinations for their classmates to try—it's not easy for students to think of them spontaneously.

Note: All of the words mentioned in this activity, as well as others listed in appendix C, can be mixed and matched or converted to other parts of speech as you see fit. Check out the "Powerful Verbs" list featuring "other ways to say *went*," for example, before directing Activity 5. Also, try combining these verbs with adverbs to further define motion: *tiptoed silently, slalomed smoothly, stumbled noisily*, etc.

Options

- Call out an emotion and ask for volunteers to depict it.
- Let students present an emotion of their choice for others to identify.
- Have students perform an emotion that they picked out of a hat.
- Whisper an emotion to a student and have the others guess what he's portraying.
- In one of the first sessions, enlist a student to help you play a trick on the class. Tell her she's going to use her face to express no emotion at all, but that her peers will be told to guess what it is. After she poses as unemotionally as she can, ask for opinions from the group, all of which will be incorrect. Finally, admit to the deception, but ask the class what it was about her expression that made them guess the way they did; it can be quite illuminating.
- When students are practicing facial expressions, cue them with verb–adverb combinations; for example, tell them to react questioningly, stare angrily, or regard suspiciously.
- Teacher, join in the fun—take a turn putting on your emotional face!

Chapter Nine

Odd Objects

There is nothing quite so humbling as trying to describe an object that's unfamiliar to you, or someone else. Your vocabulary fails, so you revert to terms like "thingy" or "doodad." Think how frustrated you get when—let's say your partner—sends you to the basement to find a tool she needs to replace a faulty kitchen faucet valve...

"Dear, will you run down and get me a faucet wrench? It's in a box with all the other wrenches. And hurry; my back is killing me!"

You descend the stairs and yell back up, "Geez, there must be fifty wrenches in here! What does it look like?"

"It's got a curvy thing on one end and a tommy bar on the other."

"What's a tommy bar?"

Annoyed, she sighs, pictures the tool in her mind's eye, and tries again. "Okay, the curvy thing looks like your curled up pinky finger. It's made of gray steel, and it's attached at its base to another curved piece of steel. On the inside of each piece are little teeth that come together, kind of like when you move your jaw up and down. The whole jaw is connected by a pin to the top end of a long steel rod, and it flops from side to side so that—"

"I've got it!" you proudly proclaim. "I'm on my way!" Arriving on the scene, you peer under the sink, ready to hand it over. "Which end do you want, honey?"

"The end with the tommy bar."

You look down. "Oh... yeah... now I get it! Here you go."

"Thank you, dear."

Details are a crucial ingredient in any piece of writing, and how better to log them into our memories for future retrieval than to be observant? It seems to come so easily for experienced writers; they pluck words out of nowhere to paint a vivid picture for us readers. We just follow along—sated—not fully appreciating how much mental energy it took to breathe life into their characters and scenes.

Young writers, on the other hand, seem to think their audiences are mind readers. They often trade attention to detail for weak, boring verbs that whisk readers along quickly, all the way to The End. They deprive us of the sights, sounds, smells, tastes, and textures we need in order to fully appreciate their narrative, and they're timid about delving into characters' emotions—perhaps better called the "sixth sense." Being observant doesn't necessarily come naturally. Teachers need to remind students of the importance of detail, give them practice noticing it, and—most important—teach them to keep an imaginary reader kibitzing by their sides.

This exercise invites students to focus on strange objects and describe them—their color, odor, texture, size, and shape—in writing. Because they're unfamiliar, they don't have names or known purposes, so students are forced to come up with *similes, metaphors, adjectives,* and *adverbs* to help readers "see" them.

WHAT YOU NEED TO KNOW

- This lesson is about noticing the physical characteristics of living and nonliving things and then describing them to others. Your students will work hard at this, for it's satisfying to portray something so clearly that others are able to envision it.

WHAT YOU NEED TO DO

Activity 1

- Think about acquiring a set of magnifying glasses; they come in handy during one phase of this lesson. (Your science department might loan you a set, but you can also find them at toy stores and surplus stores.)
- Gather a small collection of weird stuff. It's best if you can find items that have no name or identifiable purpose, but don't despair if you can't; the purpose of this lesson is to focus on details, and it's surprising how many people don't notice them, even on everyday items—the little tiny hairs on plant stems, for example. But if you're determined to go the extra mile, try the local salvage yard or surplus store; otherwise, rely on things like cut flowers, obscure tools, agates, unusual rocks, fossils, or the contents of your junk drawer.
- On Day 1, arrange your students in groups of four and introduce the lesson: tell them they'll be studying an object and thinking about how they

would describe it—in writing—to someone who has never seen it. (This is why unidentifiable objects are preferable.)
- Demonstrate how a photographer—before she takes a picture—looks at the object she's going to "shoot," stretches her arms out in front of her—palms turned up and away, fingers together, tips of thumbs touching—and then moves her make-believe camera back and forth, in and out, and up and down—until the object is right where she wants it to be when she clicks her real camera.
- Place an object in the middle of each group and direct its members to use their pretend cameras to focus on it—zooming in and out and panning back and forth. Tell them that real cameras have lenses that allow photographers to see fine details, but that they'll have to move their eyes closer to their object to achieve the same effect.
- Tell students that their objects have to *stay put* until all members of their group are ready to zoom in for a close-up view—no premature touching, picking up, or smelling; it's not nice to interrupt someone's sightline or concentration.
- As they're practicing, tell them that they'll be writing three short paragraphs—one describing their object from afar (perhaps three or four feet away), another from midrange, and the last from very close in—and that they need to *take notes* about what they see from each distance. (This final, close-in position is where students would appreciate magnifying glasses.)
- If your young Ansel Adamses haven't already brought it up, raise the issue of what to do about extraneous content that shows up in their viewfinders—kids in the background, supply bins, etc. This happens, of course, when students focus from far away *and* pull their hands all the way back to their faces.
- Tell them they should keep their object centered, but *absolutely* include things that appear around it. The whole point of this lesson is to teach young writers that, while a view from afar lets us gain perspective on life, it's but a mere summary; we have to look closer to discover the details—the nitty-gritty of what it's really made of.
- Don't let students compare notes or discuss an object's characteristics. This will be hard for them, but when the descriptions are shared they'll appreciate the unique ways their colleagues used adjectives, adverbs, simile, and metaphor to create vivid images of their subjects.
- At the end of the period, assign a due date for the completed paragraphs. (It's best to have them finished by the next day, if possible.)

Activity 2

- Starting with one group, appoint a student to parade that group's object around the room while each member, in turn, reads his or her descriptive paragraphs. (This could take more than one period to complete.)

Option

- Collect each group's written descriptions and distribute them to a different group. While your students are reading their classmates' paragraphs, pass out drawing paper. When everyone is finished reading, tell them to translate their peers' written descriptions into artwork. (You might want to supply a variety of drawing implements.)

Chapter Ten

Music Picture/Writing

Everyone loves music, and many teachers over the years have no doubt dropped a needle onto a record or slid a disk into a CD player, with the aim of calming or entertaining their students. Perhaps more than a few have invited their youngsters to draw pictures as they listened, but whether there's a branch of our clan engaging their pupils in listening, drawing, and writing *simultaneously* is anyone's guess. It's a tricky process, and the activity is not to be found in prepared curricula, which tells you something: maybe you should give it a try.

While many of the lessons and projects in this book depend on students' emotional buy-in to get off the ground, this one calls for no suggestion that emotion has anything to do with it. That said, your students might very well respond emotionally as they move from one phase to the next.

WHAT YOU NEED TO KNOW

- The music you'll play at the beginning of this exercise is *not* classical; it's electronic. The reason? While adults might listen to a symphony and conjure up images of pastures, mountains, or stormy seas, kids are more likely to draw people playing violins. Nontraditional music works well, however, because it comes from left field and liberates their imaginations.

    Note: If you are unfamiliar with this genre, or dislike it, don't worry; below are several pieces you can pull up and sample. Remember, it's not about you; it's about stimulating your writers!

- This activity is another exercise in detail, and the reason it works lies in the alien nature of the music. When students hear it, they form vivid

mental images right away, and they accept the dual challenge of drawing them and finding the words to describe them.
- For most students, drawing serves as a bridge to writing. Their visual images appear faster than they can describe them in words, so they need time to capture them artistically; the more detailed and complete their art, the easier it is for them to create an accurate written interpretation.

Note: The rare student who prefers to write *before* he draws should be encouraged to do so—whatever works!

WHAT YOU NEED TO DO

- Find electronic music: The works of composers Morton Subotnick and Brian Eno fit well here. Subotnick was a pioneer who created lots of cool pieces using the Moog Synthesizer, including *Silver Apples of the Moon*, a particularly appropriate piece for this lesson. There are lots of other artists out there though, so go online and check out samples. Select lengthy pieces (thirty to forty-five minutes): the longer your students are captives of their imaginations, the more content they'll create and ultimately write about.
- Check your supplies; kids think outside the box, so you should too. Provide twelve-by-eighteen-inch construction paper—white, manila, light gray, or even black for those dreaming of drawing in white—and a selection of tools: colored and charcoal pencils, crayons, and oil pastels. (Markers and watercolors are not recommended; the former look chintzy, and the latter are trouble.)
- Set aside three class periods.

Day 1

- Have your audio device cued up and drawing supplies at the ready. Inform your students that they'll be listening to some unusual music, and that they'll get to draw whatever images the sounds create in their minds. (Mention the writing phase here, but make it clear that this first day is about art, not writing.) Next, order them to put their heads down, close their eyes, and refrain from talking to their neighbors—all they need to do is relax, imagine, and wait for your signal to start drawing.
- *Dim the lights a bit*, start the music, squelch any whispering or giggling, and silently distribute the supplies if you haven't already. Give them plenty of time—maybe ten minutes—to get hooked, and then, in a very soft voice, tell them they may begin drawing if they're ready. (This is where a student might ask if she may write *before* she draws—tell her to go

ahead.) Emphasize that the music will continue, that there will be no talking, and that they will be allowed to share their work at the end of the period.
- Do your teacher thing: Circulate, but avoid the temptation to ask kids about their drawings if they're actively absorbed. If an individual asks if he may start writing, inquire as to whether his drawing represents everything he's imagined; if you're satisfied, say yes.

Note: Some students might ask what to do if the music transports them to *various* places—akin to dream sequences—all with different themes, if you will. They might think they should start over or use more paper. Tell them to find room on the paper they have, and that they can point out these changes in direction when they describe their artwork in writing.

- You'll be able to tell when it's time to write: unique and detailed artwork will fill their papers. At this point (about three-fourths of the way through the period), tell the class to begin writing if they think they're finished drawing, but assure everyone that there will be time in the next two days to work on both drawing *and* writing. It's important here to inform them that their final goal is to represent *in writing* everything that appears in their *drawings*, and vice versa, and that if their work is displayed viewers should be able to match one to the other.

Day 2

- Replay the music and become actively involved. Visit your students, asking about what's happening in their pictures and where the scenes are set. By now, everyone should be writing more than drawing, but be aware that many of them will discover they have to create more artwork or writing to arrive at a better match. Announce that all artwork must be completed today, and that those who need/want to write more must consider it homework.

Day 3

- Now you become a roving proofreader. The low-key nature of this project is such that you're not going to worry about editing; there's no correct format—it's almost stream of consciousness. You're looking for vivid detail, and proper mechanics. (You might take this opportunity to have students read each other's work, share their visual images, and even help each other proofread while you're busy with others.) Announce a due date for the written work.

Option

- Display the results! It's fun to feature your artist/writers' efforts in a common area. Place the written interpretations of the music in close proximity to the artistic versions, but not right next to each other; it's fun for passersby to see if they can match them up. If possible, play the music that inspired their work (at opportune times) so other students can fully appreciate their colleagues' experience.

Chapter Eleven

A Non-Essay on Elements

The world is into recycling like it's never been before; as a result, the elements that make up everything are on the move. Some travel slowly, but deliberately, like a hydrogen atom in a molecule of water that circles the world every 10,000 years. Others, like carbon atoms, can get caught in a whirlwind—resting comfortably in the local newspaper one day and finding themselves, soaked, dried, and pressed into service as a cardboard box the next. Then there are those who haven't moved since the day they took up final residence deep in the core of the third rock from the sun. How boring.

This project is fun, and a welcome frivolity for young writers, but it's also an opportunity for kids to learn exactly what their world is made of, as well as how these elements are recycled, either by nature or humankind.

WHAT YOU NEED TO KNOW

- This is not an essay assignment; the words *essay* and *elements* are merely alliterative. Your students will, more accurately, write stories about the interesting journeys that some atoms are forced to take during their never-ending "lives."
- While you will familiarize your recycling specialists with the various elements, and how they show up in our environment, you might also suggest that if they do a little research on their own they'll find more information that will enhance and justify their tales.

WHAT YOU NEED TO DO

- Set aside two periods, one to explain the activity and another for writing, but be prepared to add a third.
- A little research. Perhaps you know the basics—oxygen, hydrogen, helium, and nitrogen fill the atmosphere. But did you realize that the earth's crust is dominated by oxygen and silicon? Don't worry, though, other interesting elements, such as aluminum, iron, copper, gold, lead, and silver, live there too. And, of course, water (H_2O) is everywhere! (Although this lesson includes *some* information about the elemental makeup of things, you might want to research the components of several more natural and manufactured materials in order to help your students generate ideas for their stories.)
- A little thinking about the elements we have at our fingertips:

    - Pencils contain graphite (carbon), wood (carbon, oxygen, and hydrogen), steel (iron, carbon, manganese, nickel, chromium), and rubber (carbon and hydrogen).
    - Jewelry items are often made of precious metals, such as gold and silver, and they're frequently adorned with diamonds (carbon), emeralds (beryllium, aluminum, silicon, and oxygen), or rubies (aluminum and oxygen).
    - And then there are our *actual* fingertips: oxygen, carbon, nitrogen, calcium, and phosphorus make up 99 percent of our bodies—the other bits consist of potassium, sulfur, sodium, chlorine, and magnesium. Imagine the number of elements that find their way into (and out of) us as they wend their way around the world!

- Think, too, about the more common elements in, on, and around the earth: we humans devour them as food, clothing, and shelter, and then return them as waste; items made from them die and are reborn as something else; and some are transported by the wind—water to rain and back again. At this point, you should be ready to introduce the project.

Day 1

- Present the lesson. Tell your students they're going to write a little story about an adventurous little atom, but that first you want to know how well they understand the concept of atoms and elements, and in what form they exist in their lives. Challenge them to trace the path of a product from, let's say, mining to manufacturing—something that's made of several very different raw materials. Ask them what their clothes are made of and where those fibers came from. This will take some time, for you might be surprised by how little they know about what things are made of. Few youngsters, for example, know that plastics are made from oil (hydrogen and carbon). Also, explain the law of conservation of matter: mass can neither be created nor destroyed, so nothing disappears; it just gets rearranged—metal rusts and returns to earth, leaves fall and feed the ground, and animals turn to dust.

- Next, gauge your students' level of understanding. They should be on board at this point, but you might want to turn to your own examples of "traveling elements" to clear up any confusion and get them going. Then ask your class to share their ideas; this is a very different kind of assignment, so students will be very curious about how their peers are conceiving their narratives.
- If you sense that more guidance is needed, suggest a couple of ways students could solve the conundrum: They could first identify a common element—either in nature or a manufactured product—and then imagine where it might "go" from there. *Or* they could take that same element on a circuitous trip "backward" from its current place to others it had visited in its past.
- Finally, advise your atomic adventurers to write in the first person—it might be more fun—but to choose third person if that feels better. Also, tell them to follow the beginning > middle > end format and remember to create new paragraphs when necessary. Other than that, have fun!

Day 2

- Dedicate this period to writing, but think about adding another; some kids really get into this.

Options

- Inject emotion into the atom. Let it express its feelings and opinions about where it's "living." Maybe it feels *trapped*, or *bored*, or *excited* to be hanging from the ear of a stylish woman having a ball at a party.
- Write the piece in diary format, each entry detailing a step in the transition from one location or purpose to another.
- How about atoms crossing paths and exchanging stories about where they've been?
- Here's an example of how such a story might begin:

> I began my life inside a tiny speck in the middle of nowhere. I couldn't move because everything around me was so tightly packed and very heavy. We were all trapped—hydrogen, oxygen, carbon, and lead were there, along with some crystal-clear silicon.

Then one day there was a loud bang, and we all flew in different directions so fast it made me dizzy. I didn't think it would ever stop, but after, like, nine and a half billion years it did. Everything stopped. It was still, but I liked that because it felt like home, back in the beginning. My pals were still with me, hidden inside a very heavy rock wall. We were all trapped again, just in a different place, and we wondered if we would ever move again. But, only about four and a half billion years later, we felt some strong vibrations, and our little rock suddenly fell away from the wall. It cracked in two, and my friends were gone.

I tumbled down and then stopped again, but I was soon picked up by a strange form. I could feel it, but it was too dark to see it. It put me into a moving container, and I didn't know if I was in danger or where I would end up, but I soon found out if I hadn't escaped, I wouldn't be here to tell you my story. My name is gold.

Things moved along very fast from then on. I was . . .

Chapter Twelve

Slow Motion

A writer who wants his readers to fully appreciate a brief, but dramatic, moment has two options: he can turn his work into a screenplay, knowing that the film's editors will slow the scene down for the final cut, or he can achieve the same effect by deconstructing the action—frame by frame, detail by detail—in his mind's eye; indeed, a skilled author can thus turn a few seconds into a few pages. (Filmmakers refer to this technique as *slow motion*; author Barry Lane calls it "exploding a moment.")

Young writers need to think of such moments as a series of distinct mini-scenes. They can then stop the action, mentally, and record the details of thought and movement as these frames progress, one after another. A movie camera records mini-scenes too, one frame at a time, and the film on which they're recorded can then be projected at any number of frames per second.

An example of "slo-mo":

> My dad and I were alone in his 1940s Chevy, crawling through snow and ice, making our way up the interstate bridge spanning the Mississippi. Wind swirled over and under the immense structure, causing moisture to freeze to its concrete deck. As we reached the top, my dad panicked: Fearing we would accelerate out of control when we began our descent down the other side, he hit the brakes hard. They locked up, and the old Chevy began spinning, as if someone had reached down and twirled it like a top. The steering wheel rotated out of control, and Dad couldn't get hold of it. I was floating in a zero-gravity snow globe, looking up through the glass at an array of steel I-beams that had joined the ride. Trees on the distant river bluffs came into view every few seconds, like frames in a slide show. As the circle we were tracing widened, we began bouncing between the guardrails, and I braced myself for the cold and deadly plunge into the river below.

WHAT YOU NEED TO KNOW

- Creating slow motion is a challenge for inexperienced writers. Even when life is moving along at a relatively lazy pace, it takes a lot of discipline on their part to consider the many details their five senses are throwing at them. Now we're asking them to disassemble a complicated, fast-moving event, detail by detail; fortunately, this lesson involves a personal experience, which is easier than creating fictitious happenings.
- Details are front and center here, but not just those generated by the five senses and characters' thoughts; it's about movement. Slow motion is unique precisely because you can't hurry it. Neither can you stop it, paint its portrait, and move on; instead, it hangs there, demanding that you observe and record its every subtle, sluggish move. And that's why it's worth practicing.
- Your students won't be sure how to start their narratives. Tell them they could begin at precisely the point in time when the *action* began to unfold during their remembered experiences (Example 1 below), or they could preface it with a bit of *background* (Example 2).

Example 1

> The pitcher wound up. I locked onto his eyes, waiting for the release. My bat was ready, every muscle in my body taut. If the crowd was cheering, I was deaf to it. Then, through the silence, my coach whispered, "Don't let him stare you down. Watch the ball, man, watch the ball!" I lowered my eyes just in time to hear the slap as it sank into the catcher's mitt.

Example 2

> My whole family crowded into our van for the ride to the ballpark. It was the big game, and I was pretty nervous. Our opponent's pitcher hadn't lost a game all year, and my coach was expecting me to produce some runs. My brother and sister were trying to cheer my up, but my head was someplace else.

Note: Example 1 is probably more instructive, for young writers need to understand the value of grabbing readers' attention—the way authors try to do by nailing the first line of a novel.

WHAT YOU NEED TO DO

- Find some interesting slow-motion videos online.
- On the day of the lesson, tell your students they'll be creating a slow motion, written account of a dramatic personal experience, and that

they're about to see some visual examples to get into the mood. Add, however, that the videos are not mere entertainment; their purpose is to demonstrate that the things we *can't* see in real time are just as important as those we *can*, and that our audiences deserve to experience them fully.
- After five to ten minutes viewing samples, ask your students to think of a time when they experienced something that happened suddenly, quickly, unexpectedly, and most likely produced an emotional reaction. Remind them to be aware of the five senses as they reimagine the scene—what they saw, heard, smelled, tasted, and touched, and what they thought as the moment evolved.
- If anyone is struggling to come up with something appropriate, visit the list of suggestions below; you can read it in less than a minute, and it might trigger a better idea for some.
- Allow them the rest of the period to write, offer assistance, and assign a due date for sharing.

Suggested Triggers

- Situations that involved fear, shock, anger, surprise, anxiety (nervousness, "butterflies"), or perhaps a fight-or-flight response
- Sports: defending a goal in soccer, dribbling in for a winning layup, intercepting a pass
- Arts: performing a dance solo or a musical solo, or acting a part in a play
- First times: diving off the high board, skiing off of a jump, trying a new amusement park ride
- Scary: bike or car accident, snowboarding wipeout, getting beat up by a bully

Chapter Thirteen

Fast-Forward

Sometimes writers want to move their readers quickly through a period of time, but they don't want to skip it entirely by "flashing forward," for their readers would miss out on pertinent information and detailed descriptions of events that defined its mood. These situations call for a fast-moving summary. Think of the opening to a Star Wars episode: moviegoers sit back and watch a synopsis of a long period of time scroll up and away, informing them of important developments that transpired since they were last in the theater. (This is a device author Barry Lane calls "shrinking a century.")

Youngsters have traveled through many of these "centuries" in their brief encounters with life, but it's unlikely they've ever been asked to write about them. This exercise is their opportunity to describe such an experience and convey the emotions that accompanied it.

An example:

> The months after Grammy died were very sad, especially for me. She had been both a mother and grandmother to me ever since my parents' divorce. For days after she left us, I stayed in my room and cried, only coming out to eat a little. There were lots of people around, of course, planning the funeral and cooking food for everyone. They were really nice to me, trying to make me feel better, but it mostly didn't work. The telephone rang every five minutes, people from out of town looking for places to stay. Others were calling to say how sorry they were that Grammy died; most of them I had never heard of before. After the funeral, the phone quit ringing. I had never felt so alone in my life. It was just my mom and me, and she could only stay away from her job for two weeks. I went back to school the day she returned to work, and when I came home I would go and stay with the neighbor down the street. She was old, too, just like my grandma, and that was comforting to me. She talked about Grammy. I liked that, because sometimes it seemed like people didn't want to talk about her. I helped her with little jobs, she helped me with my homework, and

we played games together. I went there every day for two months until school was out. By then I knew I would be okay, but I still missed my Grammy very much.

WHAT YOU NEED TO KNOW

- Summarizing is an important skill that does not come easily, but by having students write a brief recap of a special segment of their own lives we can help them develop it.
- The fast-forward technique is a summary, but it's not a vague recall; it supplies information and perspective that will accompany the reader on his way to the next stop.
- Experienced writers know when to move readers forward quickly; after all, they've written everything that came before, and they know where it's headed. They also know how to transition into, and out of, these periods of time. Your students' summaries will have no context, no connection to a larger story, so they'll benefit from hearing or reading examples, many of which are scattered throughout the novels resting on your classroom shelves.
- If you encourage your writers to experiment with this technique as they produce their own narratives, it won't be long before you hear, "Ms. Jones, I know just where to do this in my Open Topic story!"
- Describing and discussing this activity takes most of a period; plan another for serious writing, or think about having students finish it outside of class.

WHAT YOU NEED TO DO

- Study the list of "life segments" below and jot down others that you think of.
- On the day you introduce the activity, start by asking your class why a writer might want to hurry through one part of her story to get to the next. Discuss their reasons and add your comments—including the difference between "fast-forward" and "flash-forward." Tell them they're going to write a life segment of their own after they hear an example.
- Introduce the example from the beginning of this chapter, but before you read it tell your audience to listen for the details that helped bring it to life and define its mood. When you're finished reading, share comments and questions.
- Ask students to think of periods in their lives that were different somehow from the usual routine, and invite them to share. (It's always best if they

can be self-inspired, so give their ideas a full airing before you resort to the aforementioned list.)

Note: Life phases of a few months are advisable, for they provide lots of opportunities to focus in on specific events that characterize a period of time; on the other hand, students often come up with compelling arguments for depicting a shorter span of time.

- Assign the exercise: Make sure your students understand that they're not to add narrative before or after the actual period they're summarizing. It's just an exercise, so it should look a lot like the example they listened to. (Tell them you expect at least two or three paragraphs—written in the past tense—and give them a due date.)

Life Segments That Might Resonate with Students

- The months before or after the birth of a sibling
- Life during a major home remodeling project
- A new pet in the house
- The death of a pet
- Time spent living with a relative, away from home
- A relative comes to live with you
- The time leading up to the death of an ill family member
- The period after a death in the family
- Adjusting to a new neighborhood, school, city, or country
- Summer spent playing Little League sports
- Summer instructional camps (language, music, theater, outdoor skills)
- Getting used to a new grade in school
- A particularly memorable year in school
- Months spent recovering from a serious illness or injury
- Adjusting to being the only child still living at home
- Being homeless
- Coping while a parent is unemployed
- When your stay-at-home mom or dad suddenly has to go back to work
- A period leading up to, or after, your parents' divorce
- A step-parent stepping into your life by moving in with your mom or dad
- One of your divorced parents remarrying, and you moving to become part of a blended family

Chapter Fourteen

Create a Life

In 1936, photographer Dorothea Lange took an evocative picture, a study in emotion that moves people yet today. You see a woman, seated, with two small children standing on either side of her. Only the backs of their heads are visible, as their faces are buried in her shoulders. Then you notice the soft outline of an infant's face—speckled with dirt, eyes closed. Its body disappears into the folds of its mother's raggedy clothes. You care about this woman, want to get to know her, but she's not inviting you in—her eyes are turned away from the camera, gazing into an uncertain future. You can't help but imagine her backstory—to try to fill in the blanks—and that's the point of this exercise.

In contrast, imagine trying to describe the life of a fashion model. You can't, for she's opaque. You see no wrinkles, scars, or signs of emotion. There's no context within which she fits, so you can't possibly care about her, let alone write about her. This is why you'll need a classroom set of photos that depict "real" people—those with a past, a present, and a future.

With only photographs as references, your students will invent characters. They'll search for clues in their subjects' faces, stature, and dress, and speculate about work history and family life. The results? Imagine finding a picture of an old codger in your grandparents' attic. You ask your grandmother who it is, and she delivers a wistful description of the life and times of your great-grandfather.

WHAT YOU NEED TO KNOW

- This piece of writing is not exactly a life story; it's more like a cross between a biographical sketch, a character sketch, and an obituary.

Note: There are two types of obituaries in newspapers. The slim ones reveal the names of relatives and the funeral arrangements but little about the deceased. Then there is the feature-of-the-day obituary—typically a thousand-word narrative extolling the virtues and accomplishments of a departed pillar of the community—which is similar to what we're looking for here.

- Old people might be the best subjects. They've seen and done a lot, and they wear their history on their faces, which can give students insight into what might lie behind them; on the other hand, there are plenty of younger folks out there who have left a trail too.

WHAT YOU NEED TO DO

- Find photos of "real people" online. As long as they are in the public domain, you have the right to print them. Subjects that are alone in the frame are usually preferable, for students can be distracted—even influenced—by people or things surrounding their "main character."
- Select the pictures you want (one for each of your students), size them to fit perhaps nine or twelve to a page—you want them large enough to have a visual impact—and print them.

Options

- Imagine you're a novelist. Write a *third-person* description of your main character (the subject). Consider his physical appearance, character, behavior, experiences, and station in life.
- The subject has been approached by a writer who wants to publish an article about her. In order to prepare, he needs her to provide him with a written summary of her life. (Write this in *first person*.)
- A variation of the above: Pretend to *be* that writer and conduct an interview with the subject. This would take the form of a paragraph-by-paragraph Q&A.
- Write an actual obituary, in the narrative style, like the type mentioned above under "What You Need to Know."

Note: The photo discussed in the introduction to this exercise, along with others taken of the same family, can be found by searching "Dorothea Lange photographs." Ms. Lange spent a month visiting California labor camps during the Great Depression. The workers there had migrated west from the Great Plains, where a devastating drought had wiped out crops, greatly reducing the need for their labor.

Chapter Fifteen

Let's Write a Walter Mitty!

If you ask your students if they've ever imagined scenarios in which they played the hero, you'll get mixed responses—some will say yes, some no, and others will just look perplexed. James Thurber, however, author of the short story "The Secret Life of Walter Mitty," almost certainly indulged in such fantasies, for it's hard to believe that even someone as talented as he could have created such a tale out of whole cloth; in any case, after youngsters hear this story about a chronic daydreamer, they'll have fun stepping into his role, if only temporarily.

WHAT YOU NEED TO KNOW

- The story takes place in one day, and it's only six pages long, so you can read it aloud and get them started on their own version all in one class session.
- The purpose here is *not* to teach kids how to write short stories, no more than encouraging students to write longer stories is meant to turn them into novelists; both represent very high bars for young writers. This exercise simply provides exposure to the format, as well as an opportunity to exercise their imaginations and focus on detail. (There is a beginning, middle, and end to this story, which you should point out, but students need not strictly follow it.)
- Walter Mitty, the character, belongs to a bygone era—the story of this man, who lacked self-confidence and was treated like a child by his wife, appeared in the *New Yorker* in March 1939. In those days, readers surely dubbed him a "henpecked husband," but the tale's sexist bent should not deter teachers. Rather, they should hit the issue head on by discussing the changes in attitudes brought about by the modern women's movement.

- Thurber's genius is in the way he seamlessly transitions Walter between daydreams and reality. While he and his wife are in town tending to weekly business, Mrs. Mitty sends him off on his own, where he succumbs to fantasies triggered by the sights and sounds of the city: real encounters ignite his imagination, and they also bring him out of his fog. You need to explain all of these transitions to your students; they won't pick up on them from a single reading.
- Most students will be comfortable with this exercise right away—either because they are a bit like Mr. Mitty or they understand him—but others won't. In either case, they need to write it in third person; after all, the actions are occurring "outside" of the writer's self.

Here's an example of a scene that might inspire a daydream:

Imagine a melancholy man like Walter Mitty sitting in his neighborhood coffee shop, gazing out the window. He sees a happy young couple coming down the sidewalk, the man pushing a baby buggy. From the opposite direction another couple approaches. Everyone is greatly surprised to see each other, so they all begin laughing and hugging, which requires Dad to let go of the buggy. Inside, our hero notices its wheels start to turn; the foursome is oblivious. It rolls slowly toward the street just as a car is about to pull up to the curb....

> Bernard jumped to his feet, shoved a chair aside, and raced out the door of the coffee shop, warning people to get out of his way. He took two gigantic strides and dived headlong at the runaway vehicle. His forearms scrubbed the walk as they stretched out and grabbed its rear axle to bring the drama to a close, the precious cargo unaware of her brush with death.
>
> The parents, emerging from the shock of it all, helped Bernard to his feet and hugged him. "Thank you, thank you!" they wept. "You saved our daughter! How can we ever repay you? What's your name?"
>
> "My name's Bernard," he said, "but you don't have to thank me; I was just in the right place at the right time. Anyone else would have done the same. You take care now, and keep your hands on that stroller."

WHAT YOU NEED TO DO

- Study the story: It's available on the *New Yorker*'s website, but you might want to buy *The Thurber Carnival*, a collection of short stories, including "The Secret Life of Walter Mitty"; in any case, you'll need to fully understand it, for your students will have lots of questions. (There are a few sound effects you'll need to practice too.)
- The day you present it, first explain some of the words that might be over their heads, such as *craven, insolent, insinuatingly, derisive,* and *inscrutable,* but don't dwell on them; some they'll get a whiff of from context, and

any others you can talk about during the follow-up discussion. Tell your students to enjoy this unusual story and not to worry if they don't "get it." Then read it—with feeling!
- Afterward, let your listeners guess what was going on in the story. Many will figure out that Mitty was daydreaming; however, identifying the *key words and phrases* that Thurber chose to signal a transition *into* or *out of* a daydream is trickier. Point these out and talk about how Thurber used them to tie the pieces of his story together. Understanding this is critical if students are to succeed in writing a Walter Mitty of their own.
- It's also good to invite comments about Walter Mitty's character traits—what he looks like, how he carries himself, and the emotions he feels, whether in or out of reality.
- Finally, remind students that Mr. Thurber led Walter through five daydreams, which required eight transitions, but assure them that you'd be impressed with three or four. (Give them the option of starting their stories in daydream mode, as Thurber did, or in reality.)

What to Expect from Your Storytellers

- Some students—your mini-Mittys—will be on board with this little project right away, for they're a bit like Thurber's hero. They'll create a character to star in their stories and take readers, complete with multiple transitions, from reality to daydream and back.
- Others will relate to Mitty, but they'll prefer to write about their *own* daydreams. Invite these students to go for it, but change their names and write about "themselves" in *third person*.
- Those who claim not to have had "Walter Mitty moments" will have caught on by the time the assignment is issued—they will jump in, but their tales might not contain many transitions.

Note: There are two movie versions of this story, one (from 1947) starring Danny Kaye and a more recent one (2013) featuring Ben Stiller, but they pale in comparison to the written word. Viewing them is certainly an option after the assignment is completed, but it might be more appropriate and instructive to have students share their stories with each other.

Inspiration

- Arts: Many students are involved in *dance*, *music*, and *theater*. Ask students to imagine being in the audience at a ballet, rock concert, or play—a performer suddenly collapses, and the announcer pleads for a talented audience member to fill in.

- Athletics: It's the big game, and you've been on the bench all season, never having had the chance to prove yourself, but then both quarterbacks get injured; your baseball team's ace closer throws up in the bullpen; or the star center on the basketball team, on the eve of the state tournament, gets suspended for reasons unknown.
- Crime: A thief grabs a laptop from a patron at a sidewalk café and begins running.
- Travel: Both pilots of the plane you are on succumb to food poisoning after eating the in-flight meal, and the flight attendants ask if there's a pilot on board.
- Miscellaneous: injured persons, fires, floods, animals stuck in precarious situations.

Chapter Sixteen

In Other Words

Paraphrasing

Almost everyone who has ever gone to school in America understands why the Pledge of Allegiance doesn't make sense to anyone under thirteen. There are countless anecdotes about people who thought they were pledging "a legions," or that our nation was "invisible." And then there's the word "republic," which even many adults might have trouble defining, as well as the prepositional phrase "for which it stands," a construct with which most of today's young writers are unfamiliar. Perhaps the paraphrased version below might help students understand just what they're committing to. Who knows? They might even become more patriotic.

> I promise to be loyal to the flag of the United State of America and to the country that it represents, one nation under God, standing together, with freedom and fairness for all.

WHAT YOU NEED TO KNOW

- Paraphrasing is not the same as summarizing; a summary of a piece of writing presents the "big picture"—the main ideas, followed by a takeaway, and it can easily be communicated orally—whereas a paraphrased version of a document emanates from a micro-level examination—words and phrases—and it takes the form of a rewritten original.
- This activity is promoted as a way to boost reading comprehension, but it also benefits writers. It forces them to study word meaning, so it facilitates the creation of *synonyms* for words and phrases; in other words, it helps

expand their vocabularies. You could say that paraphrasing adds another link in the chain that connects thinking and writing.
- This particular project also serves as a valuable history lesson.
- If you do an online search for "paraphrasing," you'll find a host of sites that cater to teachers who want to engage their students in this activity. They offer lesson plans, examples, and ideas.
- Paraphrasing is a sophisticated skill, so it's most appropriate for middle and high school age students.

WHAT YOU NEED TO DO

- Set aside five periods for this lesson, but start preparing a week or two ahead of time.
- Create groups of four students who represent slightly different skill levels. They might operate as a foursome, but they might naturally split into two groups of two as they begin their work.
- Search online for the Declaration of Independence, the United States Constitution, the Joint Resolution of Congress (1789), and the Bill of Rights (as well as the other seventeen Amendments). You'll realize right away that the longer portions of these documents can easily be broken down into workable sections for students to focus on, and that some parts (the Preamble to the Constitution and the Preamble to the Bill of Rights) could probably be handled by one student.

Note: There is time built in at the end of this lesson for students to read *both* the original texts they were assigned as well as their paraphrased versions, so keep this in mind as you divide documents into manageable excerpts; it takes a while for a large class to read both.

- Peruse the list of famous speeches at the end of this chapter; they, as well as the documents named above, lend themselves well to paraphrasing and double as valuable history lessons.
- Make copies (one per student) of the documents you want your students to paraphrase, remembering that some will stay intact and that others will need to be cut into smaller parts. This is tricky; sometimes it's hard to work on just one piece of a document if you haven't read the whole thing. Look for natural breaks in the documents themselves—Sections within Articles of the U.S. Constitution, for example.
- Search online for the Pledge of Allegiance to find its original wording, composed by George Balch in 1887. Note the changes that Francis Bellamy made in 1892, its formal adoption by Congress in 1942, the adoption

of its official name in 1945, and the final change on Flag Day 1954, when the words "under God" were inserted. Have all versions handy for Day 1.
- Plan to have two dictionaries (online or hard copy) available for each student group, and make sure they have plenty of paper on which to write notes and record their paraphrases.

Day 1

- Tell your class they'll be studying some documents related to United States history, that they're kind of complicated, and that they are going to "rewrite history" by making them easier to understand. It's called paraphrasing, and it comes from Greek words that mean to "show alongside." So they're going to create a new version of these documents to show alongside the original.
- As an example, read aloud the *original* Pledge of Allegiance; explain how it evolved. Then read the pledge we've become familiar with today and ask your students if they're unsure of any of its words. Some will come up with synonyms, which you will affirm or tweak.
- Next, switch tactics and ask your class what the overall meaning of the pledge is. Now you're looking for *summaries*, and your class will have no trouble explaining the gist of the promise; they might well offer a few more synonyms too. At this point, they're beginning to understand that a summarization is about an overall idea and that paraphrasing is more like reworking, or simplifying, a text.
- Now, read the paraphrased pledge at the beginning of this lesson and ask your audience if it sounds like a summary, or if it's an example of paraphrasing. Assuming they've gotten the idea, tell them that they're going to do the same thing with some other cool documents. (If they ask who wrote it, tell them it was a teacher who wanted his second graders to understand what they were promising at the start of every school day.)
- Announce the subject matter of each of your clipped documents to the whole class, and then pass them out to each member of the foursomes you had in mind. Tell them they should feel free to use their dictionaries, and that they might decide to work in pairs, but that the group needs to collaborate and create only one final document. Finally, suggest that they strive to make their rewritten documents meaningful to second graders.
- Tell your class to read their documents silently, circle words that they don't understand, and then talk with their partners about the general meaning (summary) of the text. By now, if not before, the period will be over, so make it clear that they will have two more periods to look up words, find and agree on synonyms, and compose a group rewording of the original text.

Days 2 and 3

- Help your paraphrasers, as this task is not easy. If they're having trouble, offer a few synonyms to keep them moving along. Also point out that they can't always simply replace a word with its synonym; the words around it might have to be changed too.

Days 4 and 5: Showtime

- Have each group select one member to read the original version of their document aloud to the class and another to read the group's paraphrased rewrite. (If there's time, invite the audience to provide constructive feedback to each group.)

Options

- Have your class work on consecutive parts of the same document; that way each group of four will produce a piece of a larger "puzzle," which becomes whole when the job is finished. This works well when a document is fairly long, or if you assign a lengthy *part* of a long document, say, a Section or two from the Constitution.
- If you think you'd like to assign roles, you could set this up as a cooperative learning experience: one student looks up words, another looks up synonyms and keeps track of those offered by group members, and a third starts writing a draft under the watchful eye of the fourth. (As mentioned earlier, you might decide to allow students to work in pairs, but they have to know that their workload will be heavier.)

Suggested Documents for Paraphrasing

- The Declaration of Independence
- The United States Constitution

    The Preamble
    The Articles and their many Sections
    Amendments proposed by the 1789 Joint Resolution of Congress

- The Preamble to the Bill of Rights
- The Bill of Rights (Amendments 1–10)
- Amendments 11–27
- Lincoln's Gettysburg Address (all of the above can be found at www.ourdocuments.gov)

- Frederick Douglass's speech "What to a Slave Is the Fourth of July?" (can be found at http://teachingamericanhistory.org/library/document/what-to-the-slave-is-the-fourth-of-july/)

There are many historical speeches that are excellent candidates for paraphrasing. The titles listed below are culled from *Words of a Century: The Top 100 American Speeches, 1900–1999* by Stephen E. Lucas (University of Wisconsin) and Martin J. Medhurst (Baylor University). They can be downloaded from American Rhetoric's website at http://www.americanrhetoric.com/speechbank.htm. (Be aware that this list is updated from time to time, so you might have to do your own search to find these titles.)

- Emma Goldman, "Address to the Jury"
- Carrie Chapman Catt, "Address to the U.S. Congress on Women's Suffrage"
- Dwight D. Eisenhower, "Atoms for Peace"
- Eugene V. Debs, 1918 Statement to the Court
- Franklin Delano Roosevelt, "The Four Freedoms," Address to Congress
- Elie Wiesel, "The Perils of Indifference," Address to Congress
- Shirley Chisholm, "For the Equal Rights Amendment," Speech to the House of Representatives
- Eleanor Roosevelt, "On the Adoption of the Universal Declaration of Human Rights"

Chapter Seventeen

Write More!

Things to Consider

POETRY

Someone once declared that poetry is the history of love. It's an interesting statement, for love is one of our strongest emotions, so perhaps it could be said that poetry is a collection of feelings; indeed, one would be hard-pressed to name a poem that was devoid of them. The expression of emotion through writing is a main theme in this book, so it might seem odd that there is no chapter on teaching poetry to children. The reason is simple: the formal study of poetry and its many forms is not the best way to introduce children to its power and beauty.

Poetry is more a thing to be discovered than learned. It comes in many shapes and sizes, and the best of it is incredibly fine-tuned. Not a syllable is wasted; it's the epitome of economy of words. It's not easy, and children are a bit intimidated by it. That's too bad, because at its base it's just observation, wonder, and emotion—with which all children are familiar.

The best way to approach poetry is to read poems aloud to your class, perhaps one each day. Don't get bogged down trying to teach too much about rhyme or meter or form; let your students hear it and grow into it. Just as you prepared your students for the memoir project in chapter 1 by asking them to describe an emotional event, prompt them to venture into poetry by asking them what moves them: the mysteries of nature and human behavior; what makes them love and hate and worry and hope; what uplifts them and brings them down—the form will follow. (Don't forget to consult the emotions lists in appendix C.)

Ironically, exposing children to free verse and rap is an excellent way to introduce them to the art, as they allows kids to express feelings and observations unencumbered by the rules of traditional structures. The limerick form is also appealing to young poets; it's fun, and the rhyme pattern is very easy for them to pick up. Haiku stands out as a friendly form as well, for it is, at once, simple and sophisticated: it requires only a description of a live moment in nature, there's no worrying about rhyme, it's short and to the point, and kids love the challenge of counting syllables. (There's also the practicality of taking an inspiring walk around the schoolyard, where the wonders of nature are impossible to miss.)

There are lots of poetry-for-kids books available, but one that sticks out is *A Child's Introduction to Poetry*, a wonderful read-aloud book by Michael Driscoll (2003). It presents 65 works by an array of great poets, biographical information on each one, and some words about the various forms. The illustrations by Meredith Hamilton are lovely, and to top it off, the book comes with a CD that features professional actors reading each of the 65 poems.

Note: Poetic teachers should read a bit of their own work once in a while; it helps students feel more comfortable with the genre, and it gives them confidence to express themselves through poetry.

FOLKTALES

Like poetry, folktales should be regarded as a way to get kids to express their views about life, not so much to study those of others. While it's instructive for children to read, and listen to, poetry and folktales, they need to be given the opportunity to create their own; having kids copy a famous poem, add an illustration, and display it in the hall is not enough. Nor is acting out someone else's version of how the leopard got its spots.

The youngest of school children, like the folks who lived thousands of years ago, wonder about why things are the way they are. Yes, they know more about the scientific answers to these questions, but they relish the idea of escaping to a more naïve period and conjuring explanations for themselves. (Older students will enjoy this challenge, too, and take an offbeat approach.)

Read some folktales to your class, discuss others that they are familiar with, and talk about why this story form might have been "invented." Tell them they're going to create a tale with everyone's input and ideas, remind them that folktale titles are usually expressed as questions, and ask if anyone has a title to offer. If so, kick it around, solicit comments, and see where it goes. Your biggest challenge will be to steer the discussion away from magical, religious, or scientific explanations for everything. If ideas are scarce, you can offer some ideas of your own, suggest creating a new version of an old folktale, or refer to the list below; in any case, jot down notes for all to see as the story develops.

Finally, think about options for publication: you could simply type it up and give each student a copy, or you could go whole hog by having your kids make costumes and props, practice an enactment, and invite other classes to come see it performed.

Suggested Titles for Made-Up Folktales

- "How Did the Snake Get Its Rattle Tail?"
- "How Did Indian Corn Get Its Many Colors?"
- "How Did Pigeons Get Their Iridescent Feathers?"
- "Why Are the Planets Round?"
- "How Did Earth and Moon Become Friends?"
- "What's the Noise Inside a Seashell?"
- "Why Does the Arctic Tern Spend Its Whole Life Flying to and from the North and South Poles?"
- "Why Are Sunsets Orange?"
- "What's on the Other Side of the Moon?"
- "How Did the Cat Get Its Meow?"
- "How Did the Owl's Wings Become Silent?"
- "How Did People Come to Be Different Colors?"

CARTOONS

Graphic novels are big, and one way to provide a change of pace for hard-working writing students is to have them produce a cartoon story. It forces them to think up a tale from beginning to end—complete with characters, illustrations, and dialogue—and depict it within the bounds of a twelve-by-eighteen-inch sheet of white construction paper.

First, decide how many frames you want your students to fill—either twelve rectangles measuring three by six, or twenty-four squares measuring three by three. But, there's another option: Give your authors room to roam by taping *two* twelve-by-eighteen-inch sheets together along the eighteen-inch side, thus yielding a jumbo sheet that will accommodate twenty-four rectangles measuring three by six, or eighteen squares measuring six by six.

Older students will be able to measure and outline the frames on their own; teachers of younger ones will have to take on the job themselves, but the results will be worth it.

HOMOGRAPH STORIES

Homographs are words that are written (*graph*) the same (*homo*) but have different pronunciations and different meanings, like *does*: "He *does* not like to shoot *does*." The challenge of creating stories filled with them—or simply a host of nonsensical sentences—appeals to the creative nature of children, and it broadens their vocabularies. In appendix C you'll find a *compact* (meaning *small*, not *an agreement*) list of these unusual words for your students to play with.

SOME THINGS ARE ANALOGOUS; SOME ARE NOT

If you teach either reading *or* writing, visit www.wordmasterschallenge.com. This organization sponsors a national vocabulary competition based on students' understanding of analogies. The competition angle is fun, of course, but the learning opportunity is very serious. While the study of analogies greatly expands students' vocabularies, it also requires them to think more deeply about the relationships between words, which even serves to remind them of the power of simile and metaphor; indeed, WordMasters helps writers as well as readers. When you visit the website, you'll learn how the competition works, view the support materials that will help prep your students for the trimester "meets," and find out how to enroll. This program is invaluable.

I HEAR YOUR VOICE!

It takes a long time for young writers to develop a distinctive voice, but it's fun to check in on their progress every so often. Have everyone in your class write a paragraph describing the *same* person, place, or thing. It could be a certain teacher or other staff member; a classmate; a well-known entertainment figure; a common space in or around the school; or a particularly unpopular school lunch.

Students should focus on behavior, style, and attitude, as well as physical detail. Each student's goal is to paint a picture in words that her classmates could only attribute to *her*. This exercise could be completed in one class period or assigned as homework; in either case, shuffle the resulting paragraphs and read some samples to the whole class. Then, invite your students to guess who wrote them and tell *why* they thought it was the work of a particular student.

This is difficult, and most descriptions will not be attributed to the right person; when they are, however, it results in a rich discussion about how, over time, we all create a unique voice without really trying to; it's the patterns we fall into that make a piece of writing our own—we search our word banks, withdraw the best ones, glue them together with just the right punctuation, and dust them with attitude.

CREATE AN ISLAND OF PROPRIETY

Don't just *dream* of a classroom where everyone enunciates, finishes sentences without trailing off, avoids lazy speech and contractions, maintains eye contact, and serves up good manners along with his good grammar—*demand it*.

Challenge your students to spend one period per day keeping these things in mind. Too many youngsters hear words pronounced incorrectly and eventually follow suit. Imagine an ELL student hearing "would of" and somehow (as if by magic?) writing *would have* or *would've* in an essay. And let's not even think about how she would interpret "Iddagoddanother one if heda gave me the money."

So set up a safe harbor. We need to help our youngsters learn how to sound as smart as they are. Who knows? Perhaps we teachers will start to sound smarter too.

Section II

Major Projects

Chapter Eighteen

Commonalities in Essays, Editorials, Research Writing, and Debate

An Introduction to Four Projects

In chapter 7 we saw how most types of writing follow the *beginning > middle > end* progression, and then invite readers to look beyond "the end" for their own, personal resolution. The following four chapters will demonstrate not only how essays, editorials, research reports, and debate fit under that umbrella, but how they share other traits that students can apply to all four, including two critical skills—thinking and organizing.

Three important notes:

1. While today's younger students are computer savvy, they can be surprisingly inept at conducting online research. The reason is surprisingly simple: When an older student or adult is moved to write an essay or editorial, for example, she consults her mental Rolodex of prior knowledge and begins to spin a web of interconnected sources that will deliver all she'll need to make her case. Yes, children possess knowledge and hold opinions, but in order to garner enough material to build a solid essay or editorial they need help from teachers, who can suggest *search words and phrases*, as well as names of relevant *organizations*, that will feed them enough to get them through.
2. At least some research is called for in each of these projects, although the *persuasive essay* stands out as a possible exception, as its supporting evidence can often be gleaned completely from personal experience; in addition, the *research project* outlined in chapter 21 is a demonstration, so the facts that students will work with evolve from

someone else's research. If students are to write a research report on their own, they'll need research tips.
3. The chapters addressing the persuasive essay, editorials, and debate do include examples of key words, phrases, and organizations that might prove valuable.

Chapter 19 describes the *persuasive essay* format—a must for students to master. Its introductory paragraph contains a *thesis statement*, which reveals what the author is intent on persuading the reader to think or do, as well as *general statements* that identify categories of *supporting evidence* that will appear—in detail—in the *body paragraphs* to follow. The *concluding paragraph* summarizes the argument that's been put forth and assures the reader that the world will be a better place if it's adopted.

Chapter 20 features an *editorial*, which is ... well ... a mutant persuasive essay. It's impatient, so it gets right to the point in the introductory paragraph by issuing a *call to action*—a plea for some sort of change—that resembles a thesis statement. It also includes an attention-getting *fact*, a no-no in the traditional essay world, where facts are confined to body paragraphs. (The introduction may or may not allude to additional supporting evidence contained in the body paragraphs to follow.)

Because this single paragraph tells the reader pretty much everything he needs to know, some refer to it as "an editorial in one paragraph," a phrase used by former *Minneapolis Star Tribune* editorial page editor Jim Boyd. Editorials begin their retreat to normalcy after the introduction—citing more evidence in the body paragraphs to justify the call to action—but they also feature a clever tactic called *speaking to the enemy*, which resembles a sneak attack: the author brings up an argument belonging to those who oppose his call to action, and then shoots them down with evidence that appears to discredit their position.

Chapter 21 addresses *research writing*, and it's patterned after the work of Thea Holtan. Her monumental achievement—deconstructing the thinking and writing process—has benefited teachers and students for decades. This writing format can be especially daunting, but Ms. Holtan has demystified it, exposed its components, and created a process through which teachers can help their students assemble a proper report, from note taking to polished product.

Now, in retirement, she has created a website that shepherds teachers through the research writing process (www.thinkingandwriting.org). As an accompaniment to her online process, this chapter presents an overview of Ms. Holtan's approach, as well as tips for implementing it.

Chapter 22, "Debate," covers a topic that isn't thought of as writing per se, yet debate conforms to many of the traits that the other three projects outlined here have in common. It requires research, note taking, evidence organization, and an understanding of the difference between fact and opinion. Each side in a debate presents its version of a *thesis statement*, moves on to cite *supporting details*, and then *summarizes* its argument, leaving the listener to ponder the *takeaway*. It's like an oral editorial—yet another way for students to analyze the issues of their time.

The four projects featured in this section dovetail nicely with one another, for they share many common elements. As you read the following chapters, you'll discover many more, and come to see them as "dots" that your students can connect, making clear a picture that was once formless.

Note: One of the components that three of these four formats have in common—the paragraph—is so obvious that it's often overlooked. Its types (introductory, body, and conclusion) and traits (topic sentences, transitional sentences, and cohesiveness) are often violated these days, so you need to study these next chapters and pay special attention to how these building blocks are formed and fitted into written work.

Chapter Nineteen

Persuasive Essay

To explain essay writing in general, many teachers invoke this imperative: tell them what you're *going* to tell them, *tell* them, then tell them what you *told* them. This is an apt description of the process, and it should be posted in every writing classroom alongside its partners, *beginning > middle > end* and *introduction, body, conclusion.*

This chapter concerns itself with the five-paragraph persuasive essay, which is good practice for young writers. Its strict format discourages rambling, it doesn't necessarily involve research, it *does* demand critical thinking, and it draws on emotion for inspiration. (If you want to venture down the online rabbit hole, you can find lots of other types to teach: personal, school, college, compare and contrast, expository . . . it's all good.)

Below is a sample essay on a topic borrowed from the Kids Philosophy Slam (KPS), a yearly nationwide essay-writing contest. Please read it, consider the bullet points that follow, and then move on to learn how to prepare your students for a similar project.

Which Is More Powerful, Hope or Fear?

Students everywhere see how some of their *peers cause others to be fearful* of them. *Dictators around the world use fear* to keep their citizens under control, and the *fear of loss* often threatens our will to go on. We all experience and observe hope and fear every day, but I believe that *hope is the more powerful of these two emotions.*

Fear of others can make school life very unpleasant. Physical bullying, of course, is the prime example, but students can also be hurt by verbal bullying (name-calling, rumormongering, and cyberbullying). These examples are disheartening, but they aren't the norm. Fear is powerful, to be sure, but friends, school officials, and communities are a greater force, and they're banding together to raise awareness of the problem, protect victims, and inspire hope; meanwhile, in the wider world, people experience fear of a different kind.

Out of fear, people in some countries fall silent. They're afraid to live the way they want to or speak out against those in power, for fear they'll be arrested. Government corruption leads to unfair treatment of certain segments of the population, and religious states dictate policies that strike fear in the hearts of those (often women) who dare to violate them. Thanks to modern communications, however, these victims know there are places where people are not oppressed—places that would welcome them and renew their faith in humanity. But there is another fear that all of us share, no matter where we live.

Loss can be frightening in a very personal way. The loss of a child can make parents fear that their marriage might die too, or that they won't be able to survive the tragedy. A person who loses his job fears a future with no place to live and little self-confidence. People with major health issues are often afraid they won't be able to cover treatment costs, or that they'll die and leave their loved ones to pick up the pieces. Fortunately, however, there are support groups, health-care workers, spiritual leaders, and community members who wrap their arms around those in need and keep them looking on the bright side.

In school, we are among people with varying attitudes, needs, and behaviors; some bother us, even threaten to do us harm, causing us to fear them. In the larger world, many live in constant fear of not being allowed to live their lives freely, and sometimes we have to deal with loss so heavy that it makes us fear for life itself. Yes, fear is bound to control us at times, but it should be temporary; often it's even healthy. But healthy fear is temporary, unlike the blanket of fear that some people use to smother the hope of others. Hope, however, is a constant, and it will forever be there for us to cling to.

Now, see if the sample reflects these characteristics of a proper persuasive essay:

- *General statements* in the introduction are there to introduce readers to the *body* topics, not to reveal any details about the forthcoming argument. Similarly, the *concluding* paragraph's general statements should be free of specific details; after all, the "evidence" will have already been presented. Their purpose is to summarize that evidence and sell the reader on the author's position.
- *Topic sentences* must also be general in nature and serve only to introduce the topics—not supply details; adjectives, however, can be used to pique the reader's interest in what's to come.

Note: Once students compose their introductory paragraphs, they're often tempted to mentally "cut" the general statements about their topics and then "paste" them into their topic sentences and concluding paragraphs. This is a difficult part of the process for them, so you need to be a coach: provide examples, like those in the sample essay, of how writers *paraphrase* and use *synonyms* to refer to previous statements; they can't just repeat the same words and phrases.

- Notice the *last sentence* in each of the first two body paragraphs. These are called *transitional sentences*, and they provide readers a glimpse of what the next body paragraph might be about. While writers today—professional and otherwise—often dispense with this formality, it's instructive for young writers to understand their purpose.
- Check the order of things. Where is the *thesis statement* placed in the introduction? Does it matter? Do the topics in the *body* of the essay reflect the order in which they were mentioned in the introduction *and* the conclusion?
- In the end, what's the takeaway? Did the author make a good point? Did he cause you to think? Did he finish things off with an eye to the future?

WHAT YOU NEED TO KNOW

- This project is about big thinking on a small scale. Young people, as they take in the world around them, ponder the same seemingly unanswerable questions that we adults do, and they welcome the opportunity to try and sort them out.
- Persuasive essays can often be written without conducting research. The topics they address are universal, and they cue thoughts, emotions, experiences, and opinions that provide plenty of grist for the mind's mill—empirical data are not of much help.
- Thirteen of the past Kids Philosophy Slam topics can be found in appendix C. For information about the KPS essay contest, visit www.philosophyslam.org. (You will find rules and guidelines there, as well as options for formats other than the traditional essay, such as prose, poetry, and artwork.)
- If there is not enough time to enter the current contest, turn to appendix C for a fuller list of past KPS topics as well as several persuasive essay topics generated by the author.

WHAT YOU NEED TO DO

- Set aside four class periods, the fourth being optional.

Day 1

- Call the class to the share circle (prepared to take notes if they so desire) and inform them of the essay contest. Even if you're too late for this year, your students will be impressed; kids love contests, and they'll start to think about their possibilities for next year.

- Have a talk about philosophy and what it means to them. Introduce and discuss terms like *ethics*, *morals*, *beliefs*, *principles*, *right*, *wrong*, *responsibility*, and *wisdom*. Then read the dictionary definition of the word and see if it makes sense to them.
- Now introduce the topic you've chosen and ask the class how it relates to what you've talked about so far; in other words, ask why it's a philosophical question. By now you've no doubt inspired much thought, so dig deeper: invite students to think about life experiences that relate directly to the topic, and then moderate the debate as they share them.
- By the end of this session, your philosophers will have begun to form strong opinions about the topic, so now it's time to tell your students to start mentally *organizing* the evidence (real-life experience or observation) that will appear in their essays as supporting paragraphs—three, to be exact. (All but one of the KPS topics force writers to take an either/or stand, as do all but one of the other suggested topics in appendix C.)

Day 2

- Download the sample essay from the *Keys to Inspiration* book page on Rowman & Littlefield's website, and have it ready to project, but start by asking a few students to share how they're coming along with organization. Then tell your class that they're going to see how a typical five-paragraph essay is organized, and that it's very similar to the one they'll be writing. Give your students time to read it, and then refer to the follow-up bullet points to explain its format and essential elements.

Note: Remember, the hardest part of this process is creating *topic sentences* in the body paragraphs, as well as *general statements* in the concluding paragraph, that do not parrot those in the introduction.

Day 3

- Project the sample essay for reference as your class spends the period writing. They are going to need your help here, for even though they've laid the groundwork for a proper essay by listening, thinking, and organizing, they now have to assemble a pretty complex document without mixing up its parts. In the end, though, your students will be well on their way to mastering skills that will serve them well in high school, college, and beyond. (Depending on your students' progress, you might want to give them another day in class before you assign a due date.)

Chapter Twenty

Editorials and Editorial Cartoons

There are many academic reasons to teach editorial writing and cartooning, but perhaps a more important purpose is served: Young people need to get involved, and we adults need to promote that. They have important things to say about their world, and though they do get affirmation from teachers and family and friends, there's something special about seeing one's name at the bottom of an editorial in the local paper. It confirms that your voice has become an official part of your community's conversation. This project is fresh and fun, and it teaches students about another type of essay format, albeit a "mutant" one.

Note: The editorial process described here is most appropriate for grades five and up, but younger students are certainly capable of writing and drawing about issues that affect them.

WHAT YOU NEED TO KNOW

- Creating an editorial requires gathering data, understanding disparate views, and learning a bit about how laws are made and policies are instituted; in short, it introduces students to a subject upon which the academic sun is sadly setting: civics.
- As students study the editorial process, they learn that things are not always black and white, and that problems are usually resolved in the gray, middle ground; as a result, they're more likely to reassess their own opinions as they consider opposing ones.
- Editorials are one more example of how emotion is a catalyst for inspiration—people don't bother to write them unless they *care*!
- Editorial cartooning is a reach for students. Expressing an opinion pictorially is not something most have had to tackle, but they'll learn that they

don't have to be artists to communicate their views, and you'll find that they're really quite good at it.
- Many letters to the editor are not written properly, which is why your students will stand a good chance of being published; besides, newspapers love to hear from kids!
- In order to teach this skill, you first have to familiarize yourself with the unique editorial writers' jargon:

   1. *Editorial in one paragraph*: This refers to an editorial's introductory paragraph, for it should be able to stand by itself. It *grabs* a reader's attention, identifies the issue via a *call to action*, and offers a supporting *fact* or two. (The call to action is described in more detail in the *body* of the editorial.)
   2. *Facts*: They can be proven, which means they can be backed up by empirical data whose integrity cannot be denied by reasonable people.
   3. *Opinions*: Opinions are beliefs—the word comes from the Latin *opinari*, to suppose. When these opinions are shared widely in an open society, they can influence its direction.
   4. *Grabber*: This is a statement designed to get readers' attention; it's similar to a "hook" at the beginning of a novel.
   5. *Call to action*: Like the thesis statement in a traditional essay, the call to action represents an editorial writer's position on an issue; it differs in that it often demands change, whereas a thesis statement leaves room for further thought.
   6. *Implied call to action*: Sometimes editorial writers hint at a call to action; that is, it's not explicit, but understood.
   7. *Speaking to the enemy*: This term refers to the tactic of bringing up an opposing view, only to shoot it down with evidence to the contrary.

Note: The *call to action* (explicit or implied), a *grabber*, and a *fact* often appear within a single sentence in the introductory paragraph; for example, "Given the fact that five thousand people per year die from dinosaur bites, it's high time we declare them extinct!"

WHAT YOU NEED TO DO

- Read the sample editorial (figure 20.1) and see if you can identify the ingredients listed above.

1. Does the introductory paragraph include a grabber, a fact, and a call to action? Is the call to action stated explicitly, or merely implied?
2. Check the introduction for general statements that foreshadow the topics to be discussed in the body, and then see if they appear—in that order—as you read on.
3. Ask yourself if the topic sentences in the body paragraphs convey a general idea of what the topic is about, without mentioning specific facts.
4. Find evidence of "speaking to the enemy" somewhere in the body.
5. See if the concluding paragraph resembles that of other essays: it needs to summarize the evidence in the body paragraphs (in order, and without supporting facts) and restate the call to action, which if adopted, the writer implies, will portend well for the future.
6. Also, notice the *transitional sentences* that end the first two body paragraphs. As was mentioned in chapter 19, it's good for students to learn how to incorporate them into their work.

- Now look at the student editorials in figure 20.2 to see what you might expect from your students. How many of the elements in the sample above are present?
- Read the paper! Clip some professional editorials and cartoons, as well as letters from readers, so you can project them in class (on Day 2 or 3). Remember, they might not be as "proper" as the ones discussed here, but they'll contain some of the key elements.
- Create a *cartoon frame*: Simply draw a rectangle on an eight-and-a-half-by-eleven sheet of white paper, leaving a one-inch border all around. Students can write titles or captions on either the top or bottom line of the rectangle, and you might want to add a line in the bottom border to accommodate a name, date, and period number. (It's a good idea to make another template with a vertical line down the middle for those students who want to draw a two-frame cartoon.)
- Go to the *Keys to Inspiration* book page on Rowman & Littlefield's website and download the sample editorial shown in figure 20.1; you'll want to project it on Day 2 of the lesson. Also download the examples of student editorials and editorial cartoons shown in figures 20.2, 20.3, 20.4, and 20.5; they will be a big help as you teach the structure and elements of editorials.
- Set aside five periods for this project, but be open to adding additional time if needed. Also, read the "Options" at the end of this chapter so you can explain them to your class.

Gun Control, a sample editorial

Guns are killing us—some thousands annually. We must come to grips with the meaning and spirit of the Second Amendment to the U.S. Constitution, admit that the evolution of weaponry has raised the stakes in the debate, and consider the possibility that easy access to these terrible tools of death contributes to the slaughter.

The Second Amendment is, indeed, confusing. We can argue about misplaced commas and whether or not the framers were granting citizens the right to keep and bear arms *even if they were not members of a militia*, but perhaps that would be missing the forest for the trees: The purpose of the amendment was clearly to allow for the citizenry to form militias, but, since that right no longer exists, the amendment seems at least ripe for review and possibly irrelevant; in the meantime, the weaponry just continues to get "better and better."

The variety of weapons and ammunition that exists today is astounding. The technology has advanced to the point where we can now buy sophisticated assault rifles, as well as bullets capable of piercing protective body armor; they're called "cop killers." And when we ask why the general public needs these weapons, gun-rights advocates respond by saying how much fun they are to shoot and collect, but considering the number of people killed by them it seems like awfully expensive fun. Perhaps, then, we need to take a closer look at how those gun enthusiasts who are *not* collectors, and who *do not* spend time at the shooting range, obtain these weapons.

Buying a gun in America is easy. They're available in shops, at gun shows, online, and on the street—not to mention through private sales. But "responsible gun owners" don't see a problem here. Yes, of course they're responsible, yet they're willing to fight for the right of *irresponsible* persons to buy, sell, and trade weapons with little or no regulation. Why? Because they're deathly afraid that regulation of any kind will eventually lead to the banning of all guns everywhere. Meanwhile, three-year-old Timmy gets shot to death by his five-year-old brother, Tommy, because daddy Thomas left his loaded gun on the nightstand. It makes one wonder how Tommy will feel about stricter gun control laws when he's a little older.

The gun lobby knows that Americans don't want to take their Second Amendment rights away. They, as well as gun owners, must also know that advanced weapon technology has largely driven the demand for stricter regulation, not so much a hatred of all firearms. At this point in the debate, the only sensible solution is for the gun lobby to support efforts to keep the most dangerous weapons out of the wrong hands. We, the people who were granted the right to bear arms, are the same people who want them regulated—for the common good and for the sake of future generations.

Figure 20.1.

Day 1

- Meet your students in the share circle and briefly discuss the meaning and purpose of editorials. Tell them they'll each be writing an editorial and drawing an editorial cartoon, and that you'll show them how to submit the written ones to newspapers. (You should consider neighborhood papers, as well as major publications. Also, if submitting letters to the editor online is inconvenient, you can have your kids supply stamped envelopes and show them how snail mail works.)

Racial preference in school enrollment

    Most children are told from the time they are still crawling that race and skin color don't matter. If true, a child's skin color and ancestry should not determine where he or she goes to school.

    Every year the school placement center devotes valuable time deciding where each child should go to school. This decision depends mostly on two things: where they live and their racial background. To comply with district regulations each school must have between 49.55 percent to 79.55 percent minority children. Segregation was horrible and completely wrong, but this approach to integration is not the best solution. Some say it makes our schools fairer for all children, but it can't be fair to send a child 20 miles away to a school he never heard of instead of a school only a quarter mile from his home, where he knows everyone.

    Is there anything different about the African-American children and Caucasian children that makes it important to have an equal balance of the two? Why not then balance boys and girls? The kids simply want to go to school to laugh, play, and learn. They don't care if the child sitting next to them is white, black, red, or green, and if they do that is where the problem is. This is not the way it should be decided where children will go to school.

    Diversity is a wonderful thing. It is all around us in nature and it should be in our schools. But it is not fair to give one person preference over another because his race fits the requirements. There are many types of diversity, but we should try to learn from them and celebrate them, not use them to differentiate.

    © 1999 Betsy Ohrn

Originally appearing in "Insights in Ink," a Minneapolis Star Tribune publication.

Year's fine as is

    Imagine yourself stuck in a hot, stuffy room at school with a demanding teacher in the middle of July. As you sit at your desk, listening to your teacher drone on and on about things you already know, you think of your friend in California, having summer vacation playing volleyball by the beach. Not much fun, is it?

    Many school officials think that a longer school year is needed to ensure that Minnesota students can compete for better and high paying jobs. This is not always true. We do not need longer school years for Minnesota students to get good jobs. Many students who have graduated from Minnesota schools have gotten very good jobs with the school year as it is, so there is no need for prolonged school years. It is not fair for one person to have to work longer and harder than another for a diploma.

    Besides, most Minnesota students would not like a longer school year, so they might not work as hard during school, making the extra days useless. There are also the costs to consider. Many schools do not have air conditioners, which are needed for the warmer days of the summer, and most school districts do not have enough funds to install new air conditioners and pay all the other costs, like teachers' salaries and extra school supplies. We should not make the school year longer. Minnesota students do fine with the current school year.

    © 1998 Cheri Li

Originally appearing in "Insights in Ink," a Minneapolis Star Tribune publication.

Figure 20.2.   Student editorials

- Allow students who are familiar with editorials to share what they've read, and tell everyone to be thinking about a topic they might want to settle on. Talk about the purpose of editorials—who writes them and why. Suggest issues that might be fuel for an opinion piece: human rights, immigration, poverty, health care, drug abuse, bullying, school dress codes, education funding. Bring up politics—the policies and laws that affect them, their community, their country, and their world.

Note: It's important for your students to feel emotionally invested in this project, so you might also ask them what worries them, makes them fearful, or causes concern for others.

- About three-fourths of the way through the period, crack open the list of topics at the end of this lesson; there's probably something there that will touch a nerve in those still undecided about a topic.

Day 2

- Be prepared to project the sample editorials that you downloaded, as well as those clipped from newspapers. (Today, you'll probably focus *only* on the sample depicted in figure 20.1.) Your task is to go over everything: the glossary terms, format, topic sentences, transitional sentences—all of the requirements outlined above—and demonstrate how they're reflected in the sample.
- As you discuss these editorials, help students identify statements of fact as opposed to opinion; it's not as easy as one might think, for editorials contain many of each, and sometimes "facts," upon second thought, seem more like opinions. It's important for young thinkers to "get it," so examine every sentence and sort them out.
- Tell your students that professional editorial writers *do not* recommend writing in *first* or *second person*: First person can be off-putting because it sounds like it's "all about you" instead of the wider, public audience. In second person we "talk to the reader," which can sound a bit preachy when advocating for a cause. *Third person* is preferable, for it speaks to everyone and suggests that "we're all in this together."
- At this point, if your students have fully absorbed the day's discussion, you could project and discuss other examples; in any case, close by telling those who haven't yet decided on a topic that they'll have to make up their minds by tomorrow.

Day 3

- Continue examining the model editorial from Day 2 if necessary, and then project and discuss your clipped editorials and the downloaded student examples of written editorials. (By now your students should be able to recognize the elements of a proper editorial and begin to think about how to incorporate them into their own work.)

- If there's time, have your students begin planning their written editorials by thinking about the research they're going to do and the three categories of supporting evidence that will make up their body-paragraph topics. (Remind them about the three from our sample: *the Second Amendment*, *technology*, and *access*.)

Note: This activity is about process, so there's no need for exhaustive research and lengthy editorials; in addition, information on topics they're likely to settle on, as well as opinions surrounding them, are easily found online. You do need to decide if you want your students to work more—or less—independently, for it will affect the amount of class time you'll have to devote to the project, as well as the due date, which you could announce about now.

- Regarding research, look again at our model. We can assume that the author searched online for the opinions of law enforcement, big-city mayors, the NRA, and the ACLU. She might also have searched online for "homicide statistics" and "gun control debate." Students, however, might not fare so well. As was discussed in chapter 18, they might need advice regarding key words or phrases and pertinent organizations.

Day 4

- Day 4 is for cartoons. Project those that you clipped, as well as the student examples that you downloaded (figures 20.3, 20.4, and 20.5). Discuss the issues being addressed and whether or not the cartoonists' opinions are clear.
- Ask your students to comment on the artwork and, if no one brings it up, point out how important it is for a cartoon to be simple and uncluttered. When someone expresses concern about not being "a good artist," explain that while professional editorial cartoonists are artists, yes, and their art can add nuance to a cartoon (a facial expression, for example), beginning artists can deliver equally potent points. (As proof, point to the editorial cartoon about school uniforms produced by sixth-grade student Justin Evans.)
- Tell your kids to hold *speaking and thought bubbles* to a minimum, print words neatly and not too large, and—most important—write the words *before* drawing the bubble around them!
- Don't get hung up on the difference between titles and captions—an issue like global warming could be expressed explicitly as a *title*, or it could be implied by a *caption* accompanying a cartoon depicting a city street under

Figure 20.3. In 1999, Elian Gonzalez's mother fled Cuba by boat with Elian in tow. She drowned before they reached Florida, but little Elian was found alive, floating in the water. An international dispute erupted when his father claimed custody and insisted that he be returned to Cuba. He later was, but only after being forcefully removed from a Florida relative's home. In her cartoon, Kirsten depicts Elian as a pawn in the political fight involving President Clinton, Attorney General Reno, and Cuban president Fidel Castro. © 2000 Kirsten Slungaard Mumma. Originally appearing in "Insights in Ink," a *Minneapolis Star Tribune* publication

water: "Bill, throw that pedestrian a life jacket!" Allow your students to be creative.

Day 5

- Day 5 should be devoted to in-class writing, drawing, and, if necessary, research. A tip here: Allowing students to draw in color can slow them down. Again, it's not about art.

Editorials and Editorial Cartoons 101

Figure 20.4. © 1999 Justin Evans. Originally appearing in "Insights in Ink," a *Minneapolis Star Tribune* publication

Figure 20.5. © 1999 Charlie Jones. Originally appearing in "Insights in Ink," a *Minneapolis Star Tribune* publication

Options

- Students could write an editorial and draw a cartoon, both addressing the same issue.
- Allow students to address two *different* issues: one as a cartoon, the other written.

- For more of a challenge, require each student to express *two* opposing opinions—one revealed in the written editorial and the other in the cartoon.
- Editorials make a great hall display, especially the cartoons.

The following list of ideas for editorial topics can be found on the *Keys to Inspiration* book page on Rowman & Littlefield's website, along with several more.

Education

- Extending the school year or school day
- Gender-segregated schools or classrooms
- Homework—should we stop requiring it?

Taxes

- Tax dollars for private sports teams?
- Should churches have to pay taxes?

Crime and Punishment

- Should capital punishment be outlawed?
- Overcrowded prisons: what to do?

Miscellaneous

- How high should the minimum wage be?
- Zoos—should we have them?
- Should pet cats be allowed to run free?

Chapter Twenty-One

Writing a Research Report

It's good for children to learn how to write a research report before they get to college, and it's heartening to realize that even very young researchers can do it. Thea Holtan has proved this over the years, and now she's made her famous method available to anyone who visits her website (www.thinkingandwriting.org). The following overview will enhance the report-writing demonstration project you'll find there, for it contains tips from someone trained by Ms. Holtan herself.

WHAT YOU NEED TO KNOW

- The Thea Holtan method is designed for students of all ages. (The *process* is the same for every level of learner, but the tasks they complete along the way vary in complexity.)
- Young writers need to feel the brain–hand connection, so this project involves pencil and paper, from note taking to final draft (unless typed).
- The mission here is *not* to teach students how to *do* research—it's to show them how to think about, organize, and present the *results* of others'. That way, when they're required to search out and gather their own raw material, they'll know how to process it.
- As Ms. Holtan created her approach, she focused on the relationship between thinking and writing—the art and craft of it—not simply the ordinary business of fitting facts into their appropriate paragraphs; as a result, students learn new ways of utilizing the parts of speech and expanding their vocabularies.
- The demonstration process on her website uses facts contained in the book *Loon Magic for Kids* by Tom Klein (1990), but you have lots of options for modeling the report procedure. You could obtain a copy of *Loon*

Magic for Kids and read it to your class; search the web or a library for source materials; or refer to the list of excellent animal videos in figure 21.1. No matter what sources you choose, make sure they're heavy on facts.

Animal Video Sources

1. "NOVA: The Incredible Journey of the Butterflies," directed by Nick de Pencier, narrated by Stockard Channing, 2009, PBS. DVD, 56 minutes, teacher script available.
2. "NOVA: Lizard Kings: On the Trail of Monitor Lizards," written and directed by Gisela Kaufmann, narrated by Dr. Eric Pianka, 2009, PBS. DVD, 43 minutes.
3. "Eagles," directed by Peter Roberts, 2009, Escape Tapes. DVD, 40 minutes, teacher script available.
4. "Loons," directed by Peter Roberts, 2009, Escape Tapes. DVD, 31 minutes, teacher script available.

Figure 21.1.

- If you decide on videos, opt for those that include scripts for teachers to read; there's a certain calm created, allowing students to relax and take it all in.
- Ms. Holtan's online process calls on students to cite more than one source for their reports, but, again, this is a demonstration; she's anticipating future student projects that will go "all the way" and include a bibliography, title page, etc. You are providing one source here, and your students will do well to complete a final, proofed report, minus the trimmings.
- Your students will need more than one of these teacher-guided experiences before they'll feel comfortable producing a report on their own; it's not easy, but they will get better!

WHAT YOU NEED TO DO

- Set aside several class periods for this project. The amount of time you'll need will depend on the grade you're teaching, the number of notes taken, and how much you want your students to do independently—it will range from a few days to two weeks or more. (Levels 1, 2, and 3 in Ms. Holtan's method correspond to grades one to two, three to four, and five to twelve or beyond.)
- Study the loon research-writing model on Holtan's website from beginning to end, and then print and gather the materials she asks you to have ready. Several days before you start the project, give your students a brief description of what's coming.

- Plan to *project* the online instructions so you and your students can follow along, no matter whether you're using content from *Loon Magic for Kids* or a source of your own.
- On the day you're ready to study the source material, tell your class they're about to see or hear a body of information about an animal, and that all they have to do is watch or listen; no taking notes yet!
- Play the video or read from your print source. Your students, without feeling the pressure to document the flurry of facts coming at them in real time, will be mesmerized; as a result, they'll recall almost everything.

Some Tips about Note Taking and Structure

- Before you start soliciting notes from the class, tell them about Ms. Holtan's warning against expressing notes as full sentences. Explain that the note cards will contain lots of facts, or "pieces," that they'll be fitting into sentences for their reports, and that a word or short phrase is more flexible than an independent clause. (The Level 3 Note-Taking Card is shown in figure 21.2.)

Source _____ Page # _____ Student's Initials _____

1. SUBJECT (Use later in your sentences.) **NOTE-TAKING CARD**

2. NOTE

3. FOR WHAT REASON?

4. LIKE OR UNLIKE WHAT?   **5. AN EXAMPLE?**
                                6. A DEFINITION?

TOPIC _____ SUBTOPIC _____
[LEVEL 3]

Figure 21.2.   © Thea Holtan

- Begin the note-taking session by asking some focusing questions.[1] For example, if the subject is African elephants, you might ask, "What comes

to mind when you think about African elephants?" Hands go up. Someone says, "Ivory tusks!" Everyone jots it down.
- Continue this line of questioning for a while, and then focus in even closer—revisit the note about ivory and ask, "What comes to mind when you think about their ivory tusks?" This might elicit another note—"Poachers kill elephants and sell them." This process generates an abundance of notes and creates a truly cooperative environment in which no one is alone and everyone benefits.
- Point out to your students that, when they fill in the like/unlike part of their note cards, they're creating similes. Take time to emphasize how important similes and metaphors are in helping readers better understand what writers are trying to convey. You *do* have to warn them about "unparallel similes": if a student follows his note "Elephants are really big!" with the simile "like my dad's truck!" you might suggest a comparison to another large mammal instead.
- Depending on the grade level of your students and the number of experiences they've had with these projects, the number of notes to expect will vary. From Level 1 students, expect between ten and twenty-five notes; for Level 2, twenty to fifty; and for Level 3, twenty to sixty.
- After the note taking is completed, go back to Ms. Holtan's online instructions and carry on from there.
- At the end of this chapter is a sample of what a Thea Holtan-style research report might look like. Notice the use of adjectives in the general statements that appear in the *introduction*, the *topic sentences*, and the *conclusion*. As discussed earlier in chapters 7 and 19, adjectives spice up the innocent sentences that inform a reader *about* what's coming without revealing any details. Think of these sentences as opinions—not things you could refute. Here's an example of a topic sentence from the sample report: "This majestic raptor builds complicated nests." It tells the reader what the paragraph is about—nests—but it reveals no facts; in addition, calling them "complicated" is not going to ruffle anyone's feathers.

Note: The italicized words and phrases in the report represent *topics* and *transitional sentences*.

- While most students grasp the idea of general statements fairly quickly, they sometimes grapple with having to be "general" thrice (in the introduction, topic sentences, and conclusion) without simply repeating the same words. To see how it's handled, turn to the sample report. First, notice that the opening sentence of the introduction is *itself* a general statement. Next, find the sentence that refers to the first topic (nests) and compare it to the first topic sentence in the *body* of the report. Also, notice how the topic of nests is represented in the *conclusion*.

Note: Tell your students that it's okay to fold two, or even three, general statements into the same sentence (see the sample report); in fact, it makes for a smoother flow. Do not, however, let them refer to topics by packing them into one sentence and separating them with commas, as if they were making a grocery list!

- Students need to appreciate the order of things—first in their minds and then on paper. In thinking about how their topics should appear in their reports, they must consider an order that will seem natural to their readers. In our sample, *nesting* comes before *raising young* "naturally," so it's referred to in that order in the introduction, the body, and the conclusion as well.
- Make sure your report writers take advantage of Holtan's Subject Synonyms form (figure 21.3); creating unique substitutes for the name of a subject is pointless if they're not put to use.
- Ms. Holtan doesn't mention *transitional sentences* in her online instructions, although the Level 3 Topic Outline form (figure 21.4) includes space for them. They help readers segue from one paragraph to the next, and, like general statements, they do not typically contain facts. (Look for these in the sample report too.)
- Consistent with the construct of beginning > middle > end, this sample concludes with an eye to the future, the takeaway that lingers in readers' minds.

SAMPLE RESEARCH REPORT

Bald Eagles

Bald eagles are amazing animals. In spring they have to work hard to get their *nests* in tip-top shape for *raising their young*, yet another challenging task that will soon begin. As the little ones develop, they fast approach the day when they will *fledge*, the first step in preparing for *migration* later in the season. These birds are magnificent and powerful, so it's hard to imagine that they were once so very close to *extinction*.

This majestic raptor builds complicated *nests*. They're built of sticks, so it takes a lot of time to build one from scratch—they have to be five feet in diameter to hold a whole family. If they're lucky, a pair of eagles returning from their winter home will only have to add a new layer of sticks and line it with a bed of fresh moss. *At that point, it's ready to receive the soon-to-arrive eaglets.*

108 Chapter 21

4

SUBJECT SYNONYMS

Student: _____
Teacher: _____
Room: _____ Date: _____

Write words that can take the place of your subject. You will use some of these words as you write your composition or give your speech. Write at least **ten** words. Then circle between **four and eight** that you plan to use. While you are writing, make a check mark on the number of each word as you use it.

Number 1. singular or plural (circle one)
Subject 2. _____
Pronoun 3. she she it they (circle one)

Action Verbs ➤ Changed to nouns

"What does [subject] do?"

4. _____
5. _____
6. _____
7. _____
8. _____

List action verbs in this area.

9. _____

Other Nouns 10. _____
"What can [subject] be called?"
11. _____
12. _____
13. _____
14. _____

Below, first list describers; then list noun synonyms.
(describers ... and ... synonyms)

Adjective-Noun Pairs 15. _____
"How can [subject] be described?"
16. _____
17. _____
18. _____
19. _____

Adjective ➤ Changed to a noun

20. _____

Write an adjective in this area.

[LEVELS 2 and 3]

Figure 21.3.   © Thea Holtan

Writing a Research Report 109

5

TOPIC OUTLINE

Student: _____
Teacher: _____
Title: _____ Room: _____ Date: _____
Subject: _____

INTRODUCTORY PARAGRAPH: Write the first sentence to introduce your SUBJECT; write the other sentences to introduce your TOPICS. RULES: 1) Write topics in the order they are listed on this outline. 2) Combine at least two topics in one of the sentences, but avoid writing a whole sentence about each topic. 3) Write topics in sentences, but avoid listing topics as items in a series. 4) Write broad ideas, but avoid writing notes that will be in your report.

_____
_____

transition to the next paragraph

Topic I. _____   **I. Topic Sentence**
  Subtopic A. _____   1 -
  Subtopic B. _____   Note #'s
  Subtopic C. _____
  Subtopic D. _____

transition to the next paragraph

Topic II. _____   **II. Topic Sentence**
  Subtopic A. _____   -
  Subtopic B. _____   Note #'s
  Subtopic C. _____
  Subtopic D. _____

transition to the next paragraph

Topic III. _____   **III. Topic Sentence**
  Subtopic A. _____   -
  Subtopic B. _____   Note #'s
  Subtopic C. _____
  Subtopic D. _____

transition to the next paragraph

Topic IV. _____   **IV. Topic Sentence**
  Subtopic A. _____
  Subtopic B. _____   Note #'s
  Subtopic C. _____
  Subtopic D. _____

Topic V and VI. - Write V - VI transitions and topics on the back side or on another form.
CONCLUDING PARAGRAPH: Review your outline's TOPICS; decide one important point about each. Below, write those important points in their I, II, III, order [a summary]. End with a punch line for readers to remember [a conclusion].

_____

'EL 3]

Figure 21.4.   © **Thea Holtan**

Raising young is hard work for both parents. After the eggs are laid, the adult pair must brood, or sit on the eggs, for about a month. The female does most of the brooding, while the male brings her food. Through good weather and bad, the eggs are never unattended. When the chicks hatch, they're very hungry, so now the adults have to find even more food. The eaglets grow rapidly, and after a month or so they appear bigger than their parents. This is because juveniles have very large flight feathers, *which will come in handy when they leave the nest for the very first time.*

Fledgling eaglets are funny. They practice flying by jumping up and down, flapping their oversized wings, and hovering over their nest, like a helicopter. Their parents tease them out of the nest by perching nearby with a tasty morsel of food dangling from their beaks. Eventually they step off and aim for the bait, crash-landing a few times before they get the hang of it, but in no time they're skillfully scavenging for food on their own. *Now they're prepared for the long journey south that awaits them—if they choose to embark on it.*

Migration poses challenges for bald eagles. The first one is the decision to migrate—or not; after all, birds don't migrate just because it's a bit chilly, but because food is buried under snow and their water supply is frozen. If it looks like a deep freeze, eagles gather in loose-knit groups (congregations) before they take off. At this point, the juveniles are now completely independent and have already gotten a head start on the adults. When the trip begins, there are real dangers to face.

The fact that eagles are constantly in unfamiliar territory is a problem, for they can fall victim to polluted waters and diseases carried by other migrating birds. Sheer exhaustion can overtake them, and sometimes they starve for lack of food sources. Like lots of other bird species, bald eagles also die after colliding with electrical power lines or skyscraper windows. *But, as hazardous as these factors are today, they are nothing compared to the toxic chemical that nearly wiped them out entirely in the midtwentieth century.*

These elegant creatures were nearly *wiped out* by man. The pesticide DDT was seen as beneficial to farmers and others; it got rid of insects that were harmful to crops and annoying to people, but it also made its way up the food chain to bald eagles—a rodent would eat corn that had been sprayed with DDT, and then an eagle would eat the rodent. It took a while for scientists to figure out why the eagle population was declining, but eventually it became clear: While adult eagles weren't affected by the DDT, their eggs were. The chemical weakened the females' eggs, which caused them to collapse when the parents sat on them. This discovery led to some changes.

Many biologists and conservationists documented evidence that DDT was killing the bald eagles; in fact, they almost disappeared completely. They, along with other scientists and activists, convinced the U.S. government to ban DDT in the United States; that was in 1972. Since then, the bald eagle has made an amazing comeback, and now this symbol of our country is once again a common sight on the lakes and rivers of North America.

Bald eagles build sturdy *homes* in which to raise a family. The eggs they lay are closely guarded, and the *hatchlings* are *nourished* until they're able to *leave the nest* and learn to find their own food. By the time it becomes necessary to contemplate *migration*, bald eagle parents know that they have prepared their offspring for that perilous endeavor.

In spite of their strength and determination, however, we humans nearly caused their *demise*. Perhaps this episode has brought to light the importance of protecting the environment for all animals, including us.

NOTE

1. The concept of "open focusing questions" was developed by Dr. Hilda Taba, a professor of education at San Francisco State University. She opened our minds to the idea that, in research, facts are not an end; they're a beginning. After we think of them, we need to think *about* them.

Chapter Twenty-Two

Debate

Intelligence Squared U.S. (IQ2US) is a nonprofit organization that promotes civil discourse surrounding the issues of our time. They sponsor live, public debates, which are recorded for later broadcast on four hundred public radio stations across the country. They're modeled after the Oxford-style debate format, and the outcomes are determined by the audience—in your case, your class. The debate process outlined here, however, strays from the IQ2US format in order to accommodate younger participants and busy teachers.

No matter their age, people have strong opinions regarding laws, policies, and regulations. When young children realize they're restricted by rules, they need to understand why they have to obey them at home, in school, and out in the community. As they mature, they begin reading and listening and forming views about their expanding world. In time, they learn that the rules they encountered in their youth have counterparts in adulthood, and that they're directly affected by them.

Although IQ2US debates are performed by, and marketed to, adults, many of the topics also resonate with young people; it's incumbent upon us, then, to provide students a forum to express their thoughts, hopes, fears, and opinions. Kids today are tech savvy, so, with a little guidance from teachers, they're very capable of gathering and analyzing facts; furthermore, it's time to bring debate—the perfect combination of research, thought, organization, and competition—back to school. Our young people deserve to be in on the great conversation that is, as always, about the future ... their future.

WHAT YOU NEED TO KNOW

- At the end of this chapter, you'll find two lists of topics—a short list culled from IQ2US debates, and another composed of author-suggested,

youth-centric topics. To see a complete list of past IQ2US debate issues, go to www.intelligencesquaredus.org.
- These debate topics are worded as proposals, or *motions*; they're declarative statements, such as "Capital punishment should be outlawed," that force debaters to commit to a yes-or-no position and then do the research necessary to convince an audience that they're right. Your class, or audience, is like a jury: they'll listen to the "speeches" presented by the two opposing teams and then try to commit to one of two possible verdicts. If they can't commit, and remain *undecided*, they become "hung" members of a jury that rules, without them, by simple majority.
- The audience-participation feature of this format enhances student interest. Knowing they'll be asked to vote for the side that's most convincing makes them more inclined to listen and think; as a result, they learn a great deal about the issue at hand, as well as a bit about themselves.
- As was mentioned in the introduction to these chapters, your students will need advice about conducting research, so be ready to point them to sources that will prove productive. For now, here are a few topic areas and accompanying key words and phrases that might come in handy as they prepare for their debates:

    1. *Education*: teachers unions; school board members; state, school district, and local school administrators; and parent–teacher organizations
    2. *Government*: federal, state, county, and local elected representatives; and federal, state, county, and local laws, ordinances, and statutes
    3. *Gun Control*: police organizations; the NRA; governors, mayors, and city councils; hunting organizations, like Ducks Unlimited; and gun dealers and collectors
    4. *Environment*: the EPA; state departments of natural resources; pollution-control agencies; farmers; hunters; and federal and state elected officials

WHAT YOU NEED TO DO

- Set aside *three or four* class periods for this project if you teach lower grades, and *five or six* for upper grades.
- Search "Oxford-style debate rules" and determine how closely you want to adhere to them. Your biggest concern here is time, which is mostly determined by the length of team members' speeches. Upper-grade students will do more research; thus, they'll need more time to present their

cases. Also, scoring debates can be simple or complicated. Here, for practical purposes, the recommended method is on the simple side.
- Consider other adaptations of the Oxford rules that are recommended here as well: Each team should consist of three students—two to *present* and *defend* the team's position and a third to *summarize* that position at the close of the debate. Depending on the length of each speech—perhaps one minute or less for younger students and two to three minutes for older ones—a whole debate should only take from six to eighteen minutes, *not* including the time needed for voting, which is explained below.

Two Weeks before You Want the Debates to Start

- Determine the makeup of your teams. Design groups of six (three to a side), keeping relative skill levels in mind, and decide which topic, or motion, each group will debate.
- Cut out small paper squares for students to use as ballots—they'll need one for *each debate* other than their own. Fold them in half and label them—on the *inside* of the fold—one half with a B and one with an A. Why? *Before* each debate starts, students will write "yes" under the B if they've already decided they agree with the motion, "no" if they've already decided they don't, or "u" (for undecided) if they're not sure where they stand on the question. *After* the debate is over, they'll vote again, and the "winner" will be the side that attracts the most votes. (Also, plan to have a timer at the ready when you kick off the debates.)

The Next Day

- Tell your class they'll be debating current-events issues in about two weeks. Give them a brief overview of the debate process (the structure and approximate length of the debates and the audience participation feature) and discuss the importance of holding debates. Next, announce the topics, explain why they're expressed as declarative statements, and introduce teammates to each other. Finally, tell them they'll need to spend time researching *both sides* of their issues *before* the debates begin, because you aren't going to tell them which side they'll be on until several days from now.

Note: If you get pushback about making them wait to learn their positions on the motions, tell them that it's good for us to consider all points of view, and that sometimes we even discover things about ourselves that we weren't aware of.

- Instruct your debaters to gather evidence (outside of class) between now and the day you assign sides. Tell them to take notes that would support either side of the motion, and that you will offer (key word) search tips if need be. Let them know, however, that after they learn which side they'll be on, they will have to work through their generic research notes to create another set of note cards to use while giving their speeches.

Day 1 (Three to Six Days before the First Debates)

- Check in with your teams as a class. Invite them to share their research progress and ask if anyone has tips regarding information searches.
- Next, decide by the flip of a coin which trio will argue which side of each debate, and announce the results.
- Tell your groups that each member will speak only *once*, and in this order: (1) a speech by the side that's *for* the motion, (2) a rebuttal by the side *opposing* the motion, (3) a speech by the side *opposing* the motion, (4) a rebuttal by the side that's *for* the motion, (5) a summary by the side *opposing* the motion, and (6) a summary by the side that's *for* the motion. (Also tell them to decide, as a group, who will play what roles.)
- Announce the time limits that you've determined are appropriate for participants' speeches.
- Tell the class how many periods you've decided the teams can have to do more research and planning before debate day (probably *two to four* beyond this one), that the debates will start the day after, and that you'll determine who's debating first, second, and so on. (That way they'll all have to be ready to go.)
- Remind your debaters to take good notes, but warn them against writing sentences or paragraphs; it's bad form to "read" your debate speech.
- Finally, if there's time left, set them to work.

Day 2

- Teams prepare, and you help by offering search words and note-card advice. This would be a good day to assign two timers—a main timer as well as an alternate to fill in when that person is debating. While you're at it, assign a ballot keeper. His or her responsibility will be to hand out ballots at the beginning of each debate and collect them when it's over.
- Plan your room arrangement—no debaters with their backs to the audience, and you in the back of the room with your timer, ballot keeper, and a surface to write on.

Day 3

- Teams prepare, and you help. If you're working with younger students, you might be holding debates today; if you are, announce the motion that your class will be considering, and have your ballot keeper pass out the ballots. Tell the audience to mark their ballots, fold them back up, and be prepared to mark them again after the debate is over.
- During the debate, your timer will cue you when to cut off speakers. When it's over, tell the audience to mark their ballots again, and then have the ballot keeper collect them and tally the results. (Announce the winners only after all groups have debated their topics.)

Days 4, 5, and 6 (for older students)

- Teams prepare, and you help. When you're ready to go, refer to the instructions above.

Options

- If you don't like the idea of assigning debate topics arbitrarily and/or making students prepare to defend both sides of a motion, you should consider expanding the list of suggested topics (below) to include those that you and your students come up with; if students are to be free to choose, they'll need lots of options to pick from. (It's another step in the process, but perhaps it would be more appropriate for your bunch.)
- Discuss, as a class, the outcomes of the debates. You could spend a few minutes after each one, or cover them all in an extra class period. It's important for team members to reveal what they learned, and for audiences to explain why they did (or didn't) change their minds after listening to what the teams had to say.

The following debate topics are from the complete list of IQ2US-sponsored debates:

1. The constitutional right to bear arms has outlived its usefulness.
2. Freedom of expression must include the license to offend.
3. Global warming is not a crisis.
4. Let's stop welcoming undocumented immigrants.
5. It's time to end affirmative action.
6. Legalize drugs.
7. Abolish the death penalty.
8. Charter schools are overrated.

Here are some author-suggested debate topics:

1. The U.S. government should provide health care for all citizens.
2. All public school children should attend school in their own neighborhood.
3. It's time to make nonprofit organizations pay property taxes.
4. Cameras in classrooms would improve student behavior and keep teachers on their toes.
5. We can't trust print and broadcast media to tell the truth.
6. Teacher tenure is ruining public education.
7. Going to college is a waste of money.
8. The Electoral College is no way to choose a president; it's time for direct democracy.

Chapter Twenty-Three

Oral Presentations

There are many reasons to require your students to stand in front of their peers and deliver a few short "expository speeches" during the year, and they're all equally important:

1. They will probably have to do a little research (on their own).
2. They desperately need practice speaking to an audience.
3. They learn about things they might not be exposed to in school.
4. They do all of the preparation; you listen and deliver an on-the-spot grade.

It's not often that students get the opportunity to learn something interesting about thirty different topics in only ninety minutes, nor is it common for them to be required to gather information, organize it, and deliver it smoothly in a limited amount of time. This project is important, and it works well for two reasons: The topics are fresh, so audiences pay attention, which in turn boosts the speakers' confidence. In addition, audience members get to observe their classmates' strengths and foibles as they parade before them, thus preparing themselves for their own moment in the spotlight.

WHAT YOU NEED TO KNOW

- Your goal is to wrap up this project in three fifty-minute sessions, but as you read on you'll find it can be a challenge; regardless, you should consider scheduling two or three of these experiences during the year—they really do get better at it!
- While the presentations themselves take only three minutes, transition time will add a bit more. Also, you need to decide how to evaluate stu-

dents who finish in under three minutes, as well as those who overshoot the mark. In the interest of fairness, it's best to penalize both—perhaps a point for every fifteen seconds over *or* under.

Note: In the interest of *everyone's* time, you might decide to cut off speakers at three minutes, penalize them two points, and move on—lots of options.

- There's a list of topics at the end of this chapter, but you need to consider those proposed by students as well; they can come up with excellent ideas. You do have to be judicious, however—a presentation about a sixteen-year-old pop star might not make the cut, but an account of the life and times of Bob Dylan—why not?
- You might have a few students who can neither think of a topic nor embrace one from your list; simply assign them topics that you think they can handle.

WHAT YOU NEED TO DO

- Tell your students about the project two or three weeks ahead of showtime and inform them that they have a week to come up with an original topic before you assign them one. It's also a good idea to post a list of topics and have kids sign up for them. (Make it clear at this point that you will be selecting speakers at random, so everyone must be ready.)

Note: Younger students might need key-word suggestions for online searches of topics.

- As you accept your students' self-selected (or assigned) topics, record them for reference. Assign a due date and tell them that as they do their research they *must* take notes (*on note cards*). Inform them that they'll be allowed to glance at them during their presentations, but that their Eye Contact grade will suffer if they *read* from them, and be reduced to absolute *zero* if they show up with a typed document!
- In the run-up to the big day, teach your future orators the six characteristics of a well-delivered speech: appropriate volume and projection, good posture, clear enunciation, eye contact with the (whole) audience, meaningful content, and awareness of the time limit. Tell them not to drift off at the ends of sentences, and to pronounce *every last syllable of every word*. Warn them against fidgeting, pocketing their hands, and swaying back and forth. Assure them that audiences are *not* put off by pauses, but that they *are* irritated by a hurried delivery.

- Transcribe the grading rubric shown in figure 23.1 onto poster-size paper. Artsy it up and highlight the initial letter of each component, spelling the word *SPEECH*. Display it in the back of your classroom to remind presenters of the standards on which they'll be graded.

Note: "Up-speak" refers to the annoying habit of ending a declarative sentence on an up tone: "I'm here today to talk about climate change? Please feel free to ask me questions?" It makes the speaker sound insecure, as if she's thinking, "Are you still listening to me?"

- Download the student assessment form (figure 23.2) from the *Keys to Inspiration* book page on Rowman & Littlefield's website and cut it in half, as there are two to a page.
- Tell students they may incorporate props, trifold displays, or even costumes into their presentations, but have a policy regarding handouts: a presentation on the reproductive parts of a flower could motivate a zealous parent to send along a fresh tulip for everyone, so you might want to nip that idea in the bud.
- On five separate sheets of *stiff* paper, write *2 minutes*, *1½ minutes*, *1 minute*, *30 seconds*, and *Time's up*, respectively. (Make the print large, as these signs will be held up by a student to let a speaker know how much time she has left.)
- Acquire a stopwatch (or plan to use a smart phone) for timing the presentations.
- Start the presentations! Grab a stack of assessment forms, and position yourself in the back of the room next to your appointed timekeeper and sign holder. Choose a student at random to be the first presenter. (Everyone should be ready; if someone says he's not, you'll have to decide how to handle it going forward.)
- Remind your timekeeper to cue the sign holder at the appropriate intervals, have him start the clock, and turn your attention to the speaker and the assessment sheet. It's simple to translate parts of five or ten points into appropriate grades, so you can easily complete the form (and even jot down a comment or two) in three minutes and enter the score on your grade sheet.
- When the presenter is finished, allow polite applause, give him the hook, and present him with his assessment form—it's good for students to get immediate feedback—while you announce the next speaker. (Don't allow questions or you'll never stay on schedule.)

ORAL PRESENTATION

		POINTS
Speak↑, Slow↓	(UPSPEAK) ⊘	5
Posture		5
Enunciate!		5
Eye Contact		5
Content, Ideas		10
Hour	3 min.	5
	Total	35

Figure 23.1. Oral presentation wall poster. Art by Elizabeth Ford

Oral Presentations

Oral Presentation Assessment Rubric

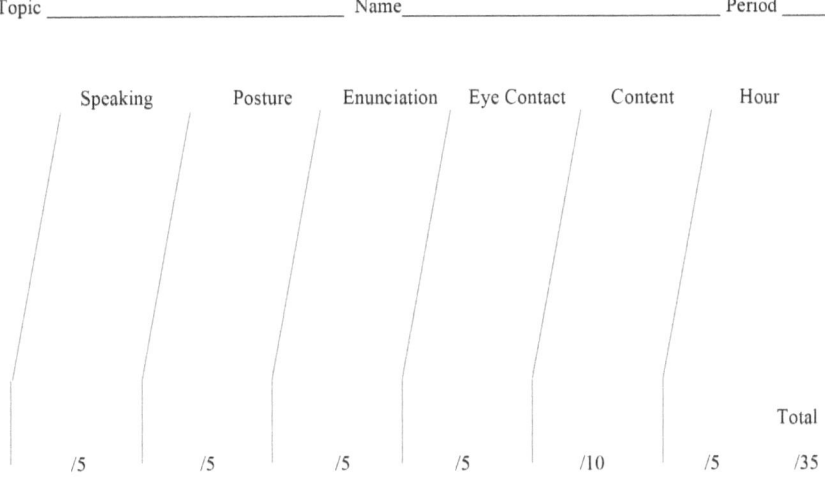

Figure 23.2.

Here are some topics for you and your students to consider, but they are only ideas. Perhaps their value lies in what they inspire, for there are limitless variations on their themes.

Inventions

The lollipop
Coca-Cola
The pencil
Ice cream
Pasta
The automobile
The bicycle
The airplane
The submarine
Guns
Chocolate

How Things Work

Water towers
Locks (as in lock and dam)
Wastewater treatment

Storm-water treatment
Recycling plants
Garbage burners
Volcanoes

Hobbies and the Arts

Coin collecting
Stamp collecting
Rock collecting
Dance (folk, ballet, jazz)
Circus performing
Fencing
Karate
Music

Unusual Animals

Bats
Frogs that spew offspring from their backs
Marsupials
The platypus
The firefly and other "glowing" animals

Biology

The skeletal system
The circulatory system
The organs
Darwin's theory of natural selection
Why animals become extinct

History

Landmark U.S. Supreme Court decisions
The Holocaust
Civil War battles
Women's suffrage
African American women at NASA
The Stono (slave) Rebellion
The Montgomery bus boycott
The Underground Railroad (check out the First African Church's role in Savannah, Georgia)
Prohibition and the driving force behind it

People

Harriet Tubman
Woody Guthrie
Eleanor Roosevelt
Duke Ellington
The Beatles
Frank Robinson
Susan B. Anthony
Anne Frank
Famous presidents

Inventors and Scientists

Leonardo da Vinci
Alexander von Humboldt
Henry Ford
Thomas Edison
Benjamin Franklin
The Wright Brothers
Karl Benz
Charles R. Drew
Marie Curie

Disasters

The Titanic
Mount Vesuvius (Pompei and Herculaneum)
The Dust Bowl

Great Accomplishments

The building of the Brooklyn Bridge
The building of the Panama Canal
The building of the Suez Canal
The reversal of the Chicago River

Chapter Twenty-Four

Technical Writing

Businesses and organizations of all kinds are clamoring for workers who can communicate effectively: training manuals must be easily understood by trainees, and office memos should be clear and concise. In a sense, it's related to the importance of detail in a story or poem, but in the case of technical writing there's more at stake; if a novelist chooses a less-than-optimum noun, it's not such a big deal, but what if a lawyer writes *in light of* instead of *in lieu of* in a brief? That could be a problem.

In the end, writing is writing, no matter the form, but technical writing—maybe the most consequential—must be perfectly accurate, for lives are sometimes at stake. Industrial designers, architects, and engineers think in terms of function, space, and movement. They conjure up mental images and think about how to communicate them to colleagues, as well as those outside their fields. As teachers, we should help our future technicians get off to a good start.

Have you ever had a tough time describing something to a salesperson—perhaps a hardware clerk who is trying his best to understand just what it is you're inquiring about? The problem could have been your description of the product, his inability to interpret it, or both. And it isn't just about calling a piece of hardware a "thingamabob" or "doohickey" instead of a wing nut or lock washer. No, descriptions of things and operations call on our ability to imagine "the whole," break it down into its component parts or procedures, and communicate it to someone else, perfectly. Sometimes these challenges even occur in outer space.

In 1973, the Apollo 13 moon mission failed, and its three astronauts had to leave the main capsule and take refuge in the lunar-landing module for their dangerous trip home. But there was another problem: the canisters that collected carbon dioxide were being overwhelmed, threatening the men's lives. There were extra canisters in the main capsule, but they were square and wouldn't fit in the round holes that held the lunar module's canisters.

Meanwhile, on earth, a group at mission control was gathering materials that they knew the astronauts had available to them (a sock, the cover of a flight manual, duct tape, a plastic bag, and more). They figured out a way to connect the square canisters to the lunar module's life support system, and then instructed the astronauts how to replicate the process on board the space ship. The carbon dioxide levels quickly dropped, everyone landed safely in the ocean, and we all learned how to envision a physical construct and describe it to someone two hundred thousand miles out in space.

WHAT YOU NEED TO KNOW

- While this project will not save any lives, it will exercise students' imaginations, for they'll have to envision and describe, using only pencil and paper, complex objects and procedures that might be totally unfamiliar to their audience.

WHAT YOU NEED TO DO

- Set aside two periods—one to explain the assignment, and another for writing—but set a due date beyond Day 2, as some students might need to do some research (checking facts, reviewing rules, confirming ingredients, etc.), not to mention the thinking involved in organizing it all.

Day 1

- Introduce the assignment by asking your techies if they've ever had trouble explaining a fairly complicated process to someone. Then ask them if they've ever been on the other end of such a fractured communication. After they've shared a few of these examples, you might want to tell them about the time you were riding your bike in the middle of nowhere and became lost. You remember . . . you asked a local for directions, which you followed, only to find out five miles down the road that your destination was ten miles behind you. (This would also be a good time to read the Apollo 13 story.)
- Explain the myriad factors that technical writers have to take into account—length, width, depth, volume, movement, speed, time, order of operations, tools, and raw materials, not to mention the conventions of their delivery system—good writing.

Day 2

- This period is for writing, but if students need extra time for research, let them do it, but then decide when their work should be finished.

Options

- Some writers are more comfortable, even when creating detailed instructions, writing in the narrative style. Even then, though, they need to pay attention to natural paragraph breaks between phases of the description or instructions.
- Recipe-style writing works here too: ingredients > procedural order > final product.
- Numbers or bullets can be used to define order too.
- For those who are visually inclined, diagrams and illustrations are a valuable accompaniment to the written word.

Here are some suggestions for technical topics:

- Recipes—a *truly* homemade pizza (recipes are great, for they can be quite detailed, as long as students don't simply copy them from cookbooks)
- Assembling or disassembling a bicycle
- Ballet positions and steps
- Board games—rules and play
- Video games, such as Minecraft rules and how to play
- Knitting, weaving, braiding, clay-pot throwing, and other crafts
- Camping—equipment, supplies, tent pitching, building a campfire
- Designing and building a robot
- Basketball, baseball, soccer, football, hockey—rules, positions, plays, special "moves"

Section III

Mechanics

Chapter Twenty-Five

Introduction to Mechanics

There are oodles of books on the market that address mechanics, which is an indication that many people—casual writers, aspiring authors, students, and teachers—need help sorting out the rules of grammar, punctuation, and spelling. But, while this book devotes many pages to this "half" of the writing process, it is not meant to be a complete guide, for as important as they are, mechanical components will never make or break a piece of writing. That responsibility lies with writing's "better half"—*content*—and students who are inspired to produce good, honest work will invest time in tailoring it, picking up mechanics skills along the way.

Call this a compact guide, one that teachers can turn to for quick reference, as well as tips on how to explain these skills to their students. Those who wish to study mechanics more thoroughly should check out *The Chicago Manual of Style*, the most up-to-date and thorough book out there.

Section III focuses on the basics:

- Spoken and written *grammar* mistakes are hindering our students' efforts to express themselves. They need to study and practice the rules governing irregular verbs, past perfect and present perfect tenses, subject/verb agreement, pronouns, misplaced modifiers, coordinate adjectives, and more. This first mechanics chapter explains these problem areas and points teachers to helpful worksheets available online from the publisher.
- Of the three skill areas discussed here, *punctuation* probably stands out as the easiest to master; unfortunately, however, these seemingly simple marks are kept busy multitasking, so they take a while to explain. Most have several distinct jobs, and the more you study them the more you appreciate the work they do. They are the skeleton that supports sentence

structure, but they also grease the wheels of grammar, put the synergy in syntax, and create mood; as a result, this is a long chapter.
- The *spelling* chapter is short, but sweet. A few of the handiest rules of spelling are explained, the role that etymology plays in expanding our word base is emphasized, and there is a not-so-subtle message to language arts teachers that we need to take the subject of spelling more seriously. Practically, however, its main value lies in the unique, themed spelling lists that teachers can access online from the publisher. Several of them demonstrate the sounds that various letter combinations make, but there are others: words that are misspelled because they're mispronounced; words that are confused with other words; Latin roots; and many more.

Finally, because this section is technical in nature, and because by now you could probably benefit from a dose of edifying humor, take a break and read the following story about a young man who struggles with the same little word that flummoxes all of us—*lie*. Enjoy.

Derek Learns about Lying; or, Let This Be a Lesson for You, Too

It's passing time, and Ms. King is on hall duty . . .

"Ms. King!" cries Ly, "Derek wrote *lyer* on my locker. I think he meant *l-i-a-r*, but I'm not a *liar*!"

"I'm sorry he did that, Ly. I'll talk to him about it right now—and his spelling, too."

Ringgg!

"There's the bell. You get settled, Ly, and Derek and I will join you and the rest of the class in a few minutes."

"Okay, thanks, Ms. King."

Just as she closes the door behind Ly, Ms. King is startled by the crash of metal on metal. She turns toward the sound and sees Derek finishing a lovely pirouette, having kicked his locker shut.

"Derek, I'm not going to waste time asking why you kicked your locker shut. You're on the fence at recess; we'll talk then. Now, did you mean to call Ly a liar? Did you write that on his locker?"

"Well . . . yes, Ms. King, but why do you say Ly's name that way?"

"No, Derek, it's not pronounced *lie*, as in to tell a *lie*; it's *lee*, as in Robert E. *Lee*, or *leech*. It's a Hmong name, and that's how you say it, see?"

"So . . . Ly is Hmong?"

"Good grief, Derek; it's December! You don't know Ly is Hmong?"

"I guess not, Ms. King, but—"

"Look, Derek, we'll address that later. For now I need you to understand why Ly feels bad."

"I know why he feels bad, Ms. King. Nobody likes to be called a liar. See, I know the word l-i-e means to say something that isn't true, and I know how to say it, but I thought Ly's name sounded the same, so I just added *-er*. It was a pun. You know, like you're always making puns in class? I thought it would be kinda funny."

"Well, I guess it wasn't so funny, now, was it, Derek? And by the way, you don't add *-er* to *l-i-e* in order to spell the noun that means someone who tells a lie; it's spelled *l-i-a-r*, not *l-i-e-r*, and certainly not *l-y-e-r*! Besides, if we just added *er* to the word *l-i-e*, we would get *l-i-e-e-r*, which would look and sound ridiculous. Now, let's get on with it; the class is waiting."

"Sorry, Ms. King, but . . . um—"

"Um *what*, Derek?"

"What does *leech* mean?"

"A blood-sucking worm, Derek. Now, why did you write *liar* on Ly's locker?"

"'Cuz he said all kids named Derek are mean."

"Oh, my, we know *that's* not true, now, don't we, Derek?"

"Yes, Ms. King."

"Do you know why Ly might say something like that?"

"Not really."

"Not *really*?"

"Noseecuz—"

"Noseecuz *what*, Derek?"

"Well, see . . . 'cuz Derek S. from Mr. D.'s class really is kinda mean, and . . . well . . . I thought maybe Ly saw what he did to Freddie yesterday. I don't know; I didn't see it, but I'm just sayin'—"

"Isn't Derek S. a friend of yours?" Ms. King interrupted. "Weren't you playing together at recess yesterday?"

"Not really . . . I mean . . . yeah, he's sort of a friend of mine, but I didn't know what he did to Freddie on the playground."

"Hmmm . . . I see, but it wasn't very nice, was it?"

"No, but like I said, I didn't know what Derek S. did; I just saw Freddie *laying* there on the grass—"

"*Lying*, Derek."

"I'm not *lying*, Ms. King!"

"No, Derek, I mean *Freddie* was *l-y-i-n-g* on the grass, not *l-a-y-i-n-g* on the grass."

"Okay! Geez, Ms. King, whatever . . . plus, Freddie couldn't talk; he was just *lying* there—okay?—with his eyes closed! It was scary, Ms. King!" Derek's eyes glistened.

"Okay, Derek, stop crying and calm down. Here, take this Kleenex." Derek blew his nose, daubed his eyes, and offered the soggy tissue to Ms. King.

"No, Derek, don't give it back; put it in your pocket! And next time daub your eyes *before* you blow your nose, okay? Now, listen to me: People *l-i-e* down. We don't *l-a-y* down. We lay *things* down, like a book, for example. I might ask you to *lay* a book on my desk. Then, later, if another student asks me where the book is, I can tell her that Derek *l-a-i-d* it there, on my desk. See? *L-a-i-d* is the *past tense* of *lay*."

"Yes, and like I said, Freddie *laid* there for a long time before he opened his eyes!"

"No, he *l-a-y* there for a long time, Derek. *Lay* is the past tense of *lie*."

"So . . . *lay* is the past tense of *lie*, and *laid* is the past tense of *lay*?"

"Yes, Derek! Now you're getting it!"

"So . . . I *lay* to my dad yesterday when I told him nothing happened yesterday at sch—"

"Oh, my, Derek. It seems you are a *liar* after all; you *did* know what Derek S. did to Freddie!"

"Noseecuz . . . but . . . you said what Derek S. did to Freddie wasn't very nice, like you knew what happened! Geez, Ms. King, I'm really confused now!"

"A teacher trick, Derek. I was fishing for information and you got caught on my line."

"Huh?"

"Never mind. Now, listen . . . after one tells a *lie*, like you did, he is said to *have lied*. If you *lie* down and fall asleep and later someone comes along and wakes you up, you might say, 'Oh, I *lay* down to rest for only a little while, but I guess I fell asleep. How long have I been *lying* here?' And the person might answer, 'You *have lain* here for about an hour.' See?"

"Lain?"

"Yes."

"But you said *lay* was the past tense of *lie*."

"It is, but there's another past tense."

"Huh?"

"Look, there's the *past* that happened *recently*, and then there's the *past* that happened *before that*. I can tell Hannah that Derek *laid* the book on the shelf and that it's still *lying* there. I can also say that it *lay* there for days without anyone noticing it, or that it *has lain* there for days, or that it *had lain* there for days before Hannah picked it up. See?"

"I think so. People can *lie*, but they shouldn't. Get it? *I* can be funny too, Ms. King! And they can *lay things* down, like books or papers—but not people."

"Well, almost, Derek. A mom can *lay* her baby down in his crib, for example, because in that situation the baby, even though he's a person, is sort of like a *thing*, because he is being carried around, like a book. The mom can say her baby *lay* in his crib for two hours after she *laid* him down, because now the baby is *lying* in his crib, on his own, like a book *lies* on a table after someone *lays* it there. If the baby's father comes home and asks how long the baby has been napping, she might say, 'He *has lain* there for two hours,' or, 'He has *been lying* there for two hours.' Later on, she might say to the baby's big sister, 'Baby Derek *had lain* in his crib for two hours by the time your father came home.' So . . . the 'helping verb' *has* tells us that something has happened in the past, but *had* tells us that something happened in the past even *before* that. See? So, if I *lie* down for a nap, I might say that I *lay* there for two hours. And then, after I wake up, I might say that I *had lain* there for two hours before the thunderstorm woke me up. The storm happened in the past, but the nap happened even before *that*. And by the way, *things* can *lie* too. Leaves lie on the ground after a storm, just like a book lies on a desk, so in the spring we can say that the leaves *have lain* under the snow all winter, or that they *had lain* there a long time before someone raked them up, or—"

"Okay, okay, I get it, Ms. King. Hey, I just thought of something! My mom taught me a prayer when I was little. It goes like this:

> Now I *lay* me down to sleep,
> I pray the Lord my soul to keep.
> If I should die before I wake,
> I pray the Lord my soul to take.

"It kind of creeped me out, to tell you the truth."

"It's okay to tell the truth sometimes, Derek."

"Real funny, Ms. King. So . . . I can use *lay* instead of *lie* if I'm talking about *laying myself* down, 'cuz it's sort of like *laying* a book down, right?"

"You're a genius, Derek, but the author of that prayer should have written 'now I lay *myself* down' instead of 'lay *me* down,' but that's another matter, and, besides, it would have messed up the rhythm of the verse."

"But . . . so . . . only people *lie*?"

"Well, of course, Derek. Fish can't tell *lies*."

"C'mon! I mean can a fish *lie* down on his own?"

"No—well—maybe if he's *dying*, but then it's not like he *lay* down on porpoise. Get it? He *lay* down on porpoise!"

"Ms. King, stop! Okay . . . a horse! Can a *living* horse *lie* down on purpose?"

"Sure; it has legs, Derek."

"So only living things with *legs* can *lie* down?"

"That's a good question, Derek; maybe you should investigate that for your science project that's overdue."

"Real funny, Ms. King, but that reminds me—my grandfather spent Christmas with us this year, and he made us eat some nasty jelly fish that he said was soaked in a chemical called *l-y-e*. What's that?"

"Well, first of all, that 'jelly fish' you ate wasn't really a jelly fish; it was lutefisk. It just *looks* like jelly, and I have no idea why anyone would want to eat it; anyway, 'lute' means *lye* in Swedish, I believe, and 'fisk' means fish. Actually, *lye* is sort of related to *lie*, Derek. You see, in the old days, when a child told a *lie*, his parents washed his mouth out with soap, which was made from *lye*, and—yes—it is a very strong chemical. The purpose was to 'clean' the child's mouth and get rid of the lie. See?"

"That's gross! And mean!"

"Well, yes, Derek, but it probably prevented some children from lying, don't you think?"

"Maybe, but . . . so . . . I was, like, eating soap when I tasted the fish?"

"Well, did you feel more honest after you ate it?"

"Ms. King, stop joking! They don't put *lye* in soap anymore, do they? Just lutefisk?"

"I'm not sure, Derek, but I think they still do. Are you worried your parents might—"

"No! I don't—I mean I won't—lie anymore."

"I'm sure you won't, Derek. By the way, in the Middle Ages, in England, *lye* was spelled *l-i-e*. That's why I think it might be related to the word that means to tell a—"

"Please, Ms. King, don't go there; my brain hurts."

"I can't, Derek; that was a thousand years ago."

"Aw, geez."

"But you *are* going to go there, Derek. Tomorrow, I want you to teach the class all about *lie* and *lay*, because while we've been in the hall talking they missed the whole lesson. And next week you can teach us about *d-i-e*, *d-i-e-s*, *d-y-i-n-g*, *d-i-e-d*, and *d-e-a-d*; *d-y-e*, *d-y-e-r*, *d-y-e-s*, *d-y-e-i-n-g*, and *d-y-e-d*; and *d-i-e* and *d-i-c-e*! You'll totally impress them with your knowledge of etymology!"

"Eta—*what*?"

"Never mind, Derek. Just be ready for tomorrow."

"Fine. I'll try . . . um, Ms. King?"

"Yes, Derek?"

"You know Bob Dylan?"

"Of course, why?"

"Well, I think he messed up on the name of that song 'Lay, Lady, L—'"

"Yes, he did," Ms. King cut in, "but please don't bring that up tomorrow, okay?"

"Whatever you say, Ms. King."

"And don't forget—I'll see you on the fence at recess!"

"Yes, Ms. King."

Ringgg!

Chapter Twenty-Six

Grammar

Grammar and its partner, syntax, make it possible for us to speak and write without sounding like we're not as smart as we actually are. Together, they show us how to assemble a proper sentence using the eight parts of speech (noun, pronoun, verb, adjective, adverb, conjunction, interjection, and article). Verbs, for example, have to be altered and paired with helpers in order to convey the passage of time; otherwise, we couldn't tell if something *is happening*, *has happened*, or *would have happened*, nor could we know if it *will happen* or *will have happened*.

Grammar and syntax help us find that place in a sentence where an adverb should be, relative to the verb or adjective it's modifying; they warn us against using an adjective that ends in *ly* to modify a verb; and they teach us that the *forms* of words—as well as their *order*—in a sentence can make or break its meaning.

Today, it seems that many of us are losing our grip on grammar. It's especially obvious when we listen to everyday people (like your students) speak. Professionals—news writers and visual media folks—tend to do better by our language than most, but they should; language is their livelihood, and they're surrounded by colleagues who can tutor them. Sadly, though, poor grammar is creeping into their arena too, and the only way we can staunch its flow is to make sure that we approach speaking and writing as rigorously as we do reading and math.

It could be said that grammar skills are much harder to teach and learn than those of spelling and punctuation; maybe that's why it's called *grammar* school? What follows are the issues that this author finds the most pesky and, like the nastiest weeds in his garden, the most difficult to eradicate.

IRREGULAR VERB TENSES: A GOOD PLACE TO START

If we all learned how to convert simple, but irregular, verbs into their past and future tenses, then it's obvious many of us have since forgotten. The verbs *go* and *run* are perhaps the most commonly misunderstood of all ("I wish I *could have went* to the game" or "If I *had ran* faster, I would have won the race"), but more and more verb-abuse victims are popping up in common discourse. The good, and bad, news is that writing and speaking in the three tenses would be easy if not for the irregular verbs that make it so difficult.

Kids have little trouble handling *regular* verb tenses—even *past perfect*—because these verb forms are the same, or nearly the same, in each tense: "I wouldn't *have hit* him if he *hadn't hit* me first!" Teachers simply need to hit the irregular verb problem head on by making it a frequent mini-lesson topic; students who have trouble with these forms will not improve by hearing them used correctly only on occasion. Even reading isn't much help, for it's passive, and meaning is easily conveyed through context—students need to learn how to convey tense by *creating* it.

Warning: If at this point you are starting to worry about your own grammar skills—maybe thinking of buying *The Chicago Manual of Style*—go for it. But as you wade into the deep Waters of Tenses, don't get pulled under by the Jargon Monster. There are words down there—present and past indicative, present and past perfect, pluperfect, future, future perfect, conditional, etc.—and they'll eat you alive.

Instead, consider the fact that most of us express ourselves pretty well, even though we probably couldn't explain the abovementioned terms if our lives depended on it. The reason is simple: we talk like our parents, siblings, teachers, and friends, for better or worse, and our writing mirrors our speech. Your mission is to create a classy classroom, where everyone learns and practices proper grammar together, through speech and writing, every day. If you succeed, your students will find their way to fancy sentence structures (almost) on their own.

But! Before we leave irregular verb tenses, consider the following explanation of present, past, and future, a major problem for many kids. Although this little lesson does contain the slightest bit of geeky jargon, it's not too technical, and it's one you could pass on to your students by creating illustrations on your chalkboard.

First, imagine yourself in the middle, between your past and future. You know that things happened in your past, but you also know that some things in your past happened before other, more recent, things in your past; in other words, even your past has a past.

Present:

I *am* at the museum. (*simple present* tense)

I *have visited* here before. (*present perfect* tense—*have* is present, so the sentence falls into the category of present tense, but *visited* means the act of visiting is completed, or made "perfect")

Past:

I *drove* here earlier this morning. (*past*, or *past indicative*)
By the time I arrived, I *had stopped* for gas and *taken* a short detour. (This shows "pasts before past," so it's the *past perfect* tense.)

So, now you can see yourself in four separate places and times *before* the place where you are now—yes? It could be said, then, that the past has "little pasts" along the way to the present.

The future tenses work the same way:

Present:

I *am* at the museum. (*simple present* tense)
I *have visited* here before. (*present perfect* tense)

Future:

Tomorrow, I *will travel* to my Aunt Marie's house. (*future* tense)
By the time I get there, I *will have stopped* at my favorite scenic overlook and *driven* through the pine forest. (This shows "future after futures," so it's the *future perfect* tense.)

Now you can see yourself in three separate places and times *after* where you are now. It could be said, then, that the future has "little futures" along the way. See figure 26.1 for an example of how you might illustrate some of these tenses.

Textbox 26.1 contains some examples of the most commonly abused irregular verbs. In appendix C, there's a chart of irregular-verb tenses for reference; in addition, there is an irregular-verb worksheet available for download on the *Keys to Inspiration* book page on Rowman & Littlefield's website.

Figure 26.1. This illustration depicts various past, present, and future verb tenses. Art by Elizabeth Ford

Textbox 26.1. Commonly Abused Irregular Verbs

- If I were you, I would have *run* (not ran) faster. (Yes, it's *were*, not *was*, but most folks are not in the mood for the subjunctive mood these days.)
- Mark would have *gone* (not went) home, but he forgot where he lived.
- I know I should have *written* (not wrote) more, Ms. Smith, but I ran out of words in my head.
- I might have *done* (not did) a better job if I had spent more time preparing.
- Tom would have *given* (not gave) me more help had he had more time.
- Laura could have *swum* (not swam) farther if it hadn't been so windy that day.
- Those bells have *rung* (not rang) for hours; I'm going crazy!
- By the time we get there, we will have *driven* (not drove) five hundred miles.
- The principal has *spoken* (not spoke), so the issue is settled.
- Our swim team's diver has *dived* (not dove) his last dive.

SUBJECT–VERB AGREEMENT

Problems abound here, too, and most of the blame for the "disagreements" goes to the *prepositional phrase*. Were you uncomfortable with the word *goes* in that sentence? If you were, you're not alone. It's a strange phenomenon, for no one would accept the clause "most of the *blame go* to the prepositional phrase." It's as if some readers and writers mentally match the noun at the end of the prepositional phrase with the verb that follows it. After all, *disagreements* don't *goes*; they *go*! Student writers, however, often key on the plural noun and automatically create a plural verb to go with it.

Note: This tendency is stronger if the prepositional phrase is lengthy, presumably because writers have more time to forget whether the noun was singular or plural: "The fact that the jewels were found under his bed during a search of his belongings indicates he is guilty."

Troublesome Subject–Verb Agreement

The None-of-Us-Are-Perfect Problem

There once was a teacher who wrote, "None of us is perfect," on her chalkboard during a parent open house. She asked the attendees if the statement demonstrated proper grammar, and none thought it was correct. No surprise there, for lots of people nowadays have accepted the idea that plural pronouns can go with singular nouns: "*Any* student should feel safe in *their* school," or "The *soldier* discharged *their* weapon." *None, nobody, any, anyone, either,* and *neither* often fit the bill too. Perhaps it won't be long before "*Any one* of you *are* eligible for the prize" will join in the fun.

The weird thing about "None of us *are* perfect," though, is that the speaker utters "are" immediately after "us" and doesn't think it sounds awkward. Really? Us *are*? Further, she can't even use the excuse that the noun and verb are so far apart that she lost track of the tense she started with!

Note: None is short for "no one," and no one would say, "No one *are* perfect," or would he? As ever, the answer is practice, practice, practice, so here are some examples:

At the party, none of the singles was interested in any other.
Is any of you going to the party?

The British Are Coming!

The Brits, as well as those schooled in their version of English, are in the habit of mismatching subjects and verbs. It's a quaint and quirky tradition that the rest of the world tolerates willingly, probably because the idea does make some sense. The thinking is that groups are composed of individuals, so what to Americans, for example, is an "it" becomes a "they" in Britain.

American example: Our team *was* victorious.
British examples: Our team *were* victorious. The government *are* meeting. The royal family *are* vacationing. The corporation's board *are* united on the issue.

Presumably, this construction is based on the notion that we need to acknowledge the human side of any organization; that it is they who are responsible for its actions, good or bad. Rather a good idea, wouldn't you say, old boy?

WHO OR WHOM

This one seems easy, but the fact that so many of us don't get it says otherwise. The standard explanation for which pronoun to use goes something like this: When in doubt, replace the word *who* with he, she, or they and see how it sounds. Similarly, replace the word *whom* with him, her, or them. (When testing for *they* or *them*, one has to mentally make the *being verb* plural.)

Ex: Whom (or who) is going to the party? *Him* is going, *her* is going, *them* are going? No, these just don't sound right, so use *Who*.
Ex: With who (or whom) are you going to the party? I'm going with *he*, I'm going with *she*, I'm going with *they*? No, those options sound silly, so use *whom*.

Note: There are worksheets dealing with these and other pronouns on the *Keys to Inspiration* book page on Rowman & Littlefield's website, but again, this is not a grammar book; you might need to consult other guides for more thorough treatments of the issues covered here.

PRONOUNS THAT PRECEDE WHICH, WHOM, AND WHOSE

These relative possessive pronouns offer a novel way to combine sentences, demonstrate a command of the language, and help to conserve words. Students learn this construction quite readily, and they soon find out that it impresses readers.

Ex: Two tornadoes ripped through town last night. One of them was an F2.
Alternative: Two tornadoes ripped through town last night, one *of which* was an F2.
Ex: Mary traveled to New York with her friend Carol. They always had fun together.

Alternative: Mary traveled to New York with her friend Carol, *with whom* she always had fun.

Ex: Mohammed was out of work. He would still be if his dad's friend hadn't offered him a job.

Alternative: Mohammed is very grateful to his father's friend, *without whose* help he would still be unemployed.

PARALLEL STRUCTURE

Children have trouble understanding how a rule about word endings and word choice has anything to do with math, so you will have to explain that the best way you can. It might help to tell your students that the word *parallel* comes from two Greek words: *para*, meaning "beside," and *allelon*, meaning "of one another." You could also tell them that parallel structure is composed of a series of related words or phrases; meanwhile, here are some examples, starting with a parallel that dictates word endings:

Ex: I will be clean*ing* the camp stove, buy*ing* a new cooler, and waterproof our tent. (See? You were expecting waterproof*ing*.)

Ex: Alicia was the reason her school newspaper succeeded: she wrote, edited, and proofread most of every issue. (These three tasks are in the past tense, and they also follow the order in which writers operate—write, edit, proofread.)

Now, these two examples demonstrate the need for parallel word endings, but they're parallel in content as well—camping is the connection in the first, and Alicia's school newspaper involvement predicted the tasks listed in the second—but here is an example of a sentence that fails on both counts:

Ex: Martin is a lawyer for the school district and his church, and volunteered at the food shelf.

The first clause is in the present tense, but the second clause is in the past; further, the first clause is about Martin's law work, and the second is about volunteering.

Sometimes a progression of words creates a parallel construction:

Ex: I want to know everything that went on in that office—the good, the bad, and the ugly.

At other times it's achieved through repetition:

Ex: You'll do well because you're smart, you're talented, and you're dedicated.

Ex: You'll apologize, you'll make amends, and you'll change your behavior.

COORDINATE ADJECTIVES AND THOSE THAT ARE NOT

First, let's define *coordinate*: it means that things are *of the same importance*. When we use more than one adjective to modify a noun, we have to decide if they are of equal importance. Why? Because if they are, we need to separate them with a comma *or* the word *and*. Consider this sentence: "My mom bought me a handmade, light red dress." It's easy to see that *handmade* and *light red* are very different; they're separate, but equally important. They deserve their respective spaces, which are defined by the comma.

Obviously, then, if the sentence had read, "My mom bought me a light red dress," *light* and *red* would *not* be separated, because one is just embellishing the other—they're not equal in importance.

Note: To determine if a comma is needed to separate two adjectives that modify the same noun, see if the word *and* could be comfortably placed between them. If so, then a comma is needed. But be aware that at times—perhaps for emphasis—it might be preferable to use the word *and* instead of a comma: "She was a skillful and dedicated doctor."

Kids can have a hard time with this, so consider the examples below and see if the commas, or lack thereof, make sense. (They should.)

Ex: Julia couldn't wait to drive her dad's new, expensive sports car.
Ex: The ball of twisted, yellow yarn couldn't be undone.
Ex: After the flood, we recovered my dirty, torn coat.
Ex: Our house has stained cedar siding.

ADJECTIVES ENDING IN -LY THAT ARE MISTAKEN FOR ADVERBS

While there are a lot of adjectives that could possibly be expressed as adverbs, there are relatively few that are *likely* to show up regularly in student writing; on the other hand, the difference between authentic and bogus adverbs is pretty easily explained, so it's worth your time to address it. Look at the example sentences below and consider using them to create a wall chart for student reference.

Wrong: "Please walk *orderly* through halls," the principal pleaded over the PA.
Better: "Please walk through the halls in an *orderly* manner." (Orderly modifies *manner*, so it's an adjective.)
Wrong: Molly treated her so *lovely*.
Better: She received such *lovely* treatment from Molly.
Also better: Molly treated her *lovingly*. (*Lovely* is changed to an *actual adverb* that expresses the intended sentiment more properly.)

Wrong: He walked *friendly* up to me and said, "Hello."
Better: He seemed *friendly* as he walked up to me and said, "Hello."
Wrong: Sam backed up *cowardly*, turned around, and ran.
Better: Sam looked *cowardly* as he backed up and ran away.
Wrong: The hikers headed *northerly* into the wilderness.
Better: The hikers' plan was to head out in a *northerly* direction, into the wild. (*Note: Southerly, easterly,* and *westerly* are equally likely to be used improperly.)
Wrong: Our teacher said to turn in our assignments *timely*.
Better: Our teacher said we'd better be *timely* about turning in assignments.
Wrong: Our teacher also said we'd better not behave *unruly*.
Better: Our teacher said that *unruly* behavior will not be tolerated.
Wrong: Thao acted *lonely* all week at camp.
Better: Thao felt *lonely* all week at camp.
Wrong: The actors moved *lively* all over the stage.
Better: It was a *lively* group of actors that moved about the stage.

Note: If you're so moved, search "words ending in -ly that are not adverbs" for more examples.

MISPLACED MODIFIERS

"Throw the cow over the fence some hay." Back in the day, this was the example that teachers used to define the problem. It worked, too, probably because it conjured up a ridiculous image in kids' minds. Perhaps today's equivalent might be, "We showered Mike at his house with birthday gifts."

The modifiers in the above two examples (*over the fence* and *at his house*) are meant to add some detail—now the reader knows *where* the cow is and *where* Mike is. They are misplaced, of course, so the reader thinks a cow is being thrown over a fence before he reads the rest of the sentence; likewise, in Mike's case, it looks at first glance like a bunch of friends came over to Mike's and, well, gave him a shower. Read the following examples to your class; if they become aware of how easy it is to fall into this trap, they might be more careful.

Wrong: High up in the tree, Billy watched as the eagles built their nest.
Better: Billy watched as the eagles built their nest high up in the tree.
Wrong: Looking up, the tree appeared to touch the sky.
Better: As I looked up, the tree appeared to touch the sky.

MISPLACED ADVERBS

Adverbs can be misplaced, just like adjectives, and it's all about the natural flow of information, as always. Just as certain words in a sentence take priority over others, the order in which they appear is also crucial. Here are some examples:

Wrong: You need to *examine thoroughly* the contents of the trashcan.
Better: You need to examine the contents of the trashcan *thoroughly*. (Why tell someone *how well* he has to examine something *before* he knows what it is?)
Wrong: We need to again go over the report.
Better: We need to go over the report again. (Again, these people need to know what the speaker is talking about (the report) before they learn that they have to take a second look at it.)

Note: This is somewhat related to the discussion about coordinate adjectives earlier in this chapter; in both cases, we see that the order of words can either facilitate or disrupt the flow of information. Also, the subjects of dependent clauses and coordinate conjunctions are intertwined, for they involve punctuation as well as grammar issues; you can find this discussion in chapter 27 on punctuation.

Chapter Twenty-Seven

Punctuation, Clauses, and Sentence Types

This chapter centers on punctuation, but an understanding of *clauses* and *sentences* is a necessary prelude to the study of these queer little symbols, for punctuation allows us to stretch them, shrink them, link them together, and pull them apart. Each mark has a unique purpose, and without them we would be limited to reading the simplest of sentences, which would make for a boring and bumpy ride indeed.

CLAUSES

A *clause* is a group of words that includes a *subject* (noun) and a *predicate* (verb); it can be either *independent* or *dependent*; it depends . . .

An *independent clause* stands by itself as a complete thought, or sentence.

Ex: Our whole family is going to have a picnic.
Ex: The weather is friendly.

A *dependent clause* is sometimes called a *subordinate* clause. Think of a subordinate employee—he is dependent on his boss for direction.

Using our picnic scenario, if we use the *coordinate conjunction* "if" at the beginning of the second example (turning it into a dependent clause) and then combine the two clauses, we now have *one sentence* with a main (independent) clause *and* a dependent clause: "Our whole family is going to have a picnic if the weather is friendly." We could also turn the sentence around, in which case we would place a comma *after* the dependent clause: "If the weather is friendly, our whole family is going to have a picnic."

Note: Some other subordinate conjunctions are *that, who, where, because, while, although, since,* and *when.*

SENTENCES

The Four Types of Sentences

The terms *subject* and *noun* are synonymous, as are *verb* and *predicate*. A noun by itself is called a *simple subject* and only becomes a *complete subject* when words around it are included. Similarly, a verb by itself is a *simple predicate*, but becomes a *complete predicate* when combined with the words around it. In the example below, "My friend" is the complete subject, and "is writing a book" is the complete predicate.

A *simple* sentence is an independent clause; it has one subject and one predicate, and it represents a complete thought.

Ex: My friend is writing a book.

Note: A sentence can be complete even without a named subject: *Write your book!* (The subject "you" is *understood*.)

A *compound* sentence has *two* independent clauses, but they're connected by a coordinating conjunction.

Ex: My friend is writing a book, *and* he thinks it will sell a million copies.

A *complex* sentence contains a main clause and a dependent clause.

Ex: Because my friend thinks it will make him rich, he is writing a book.

A *compound-complex* sentence contains *at least two* independent clauses and *at least one* dependent clause.

Ex: My friend is writing a book because he thinks it will make him rich, but his friends think he's a fool.

The Four Moods of Sentences

1. Declarative: It comes from the word *declare*, which means to make known, or to state.

    Ex: The sky is looking kind of green.

2. Interrogative: It comes from the word *interrogate*, which means to question.

    Ex: Do you think there will be a storm?

3. Imperative: It comes from the Latin word *imperare*, which means to command or order.

Ex: Yes, now go to the basement.

4. Exclamatory: It comes from the word *exclaim*, which means to cry out suddenly.

   Ex: Holy buckets! There's a funnel cloud coming!

END MARKS

The Period (.)

It's like a stop sign; it marks the end of a complete thought, but only those that take the form of a *declarative* or *imperative* sentence. When spoken, these sentences should sound final—the voice should *drop in tone* at the end.

Ex: The weather is lousy today.
Ex: Bring a rain jacket.

The period is also used after initials (John F. Kennedy) and after abbreviations (Dept. of Defense or Mrs. Kennedy).

Note: A period is *not* used after an acronym, such as AARP, or after an abbreviation that ends a sentence ("Be sure to pack cooking utensils, plates, silverware, etc."). We *do* need to place a period after an ellipsis that *ends* a sentence, however: his speech started out, "Thank you for inviting me here today. I am honored to speak to you about. . . ."

Periods are also used to separate dollars from cents ($99.99) and decimals from whole numbers (99.99 percent certain).

The Question Mark (?)

A question mark ends an *interrogative* sentence and seeks information; it resembles the raised eyebrow of someone who's questioning something he just heard.

Ex: Are you sure the product will be ready for market soon?

A question mark can also be injected into a sentence to express doubt:

Ex: In three to five days (?) we should be good to go.

Note: It's tempting to place a question mark at the end of a sentence that is *not* interrogative but feels like it is. The classic example is "Guess what?" (This sentence is actually imperative, for it simply *orders* someone to guess something.) Many speakers nowadays are also adding questions onto the ends of declarative sentences:

Ex: It's time to discuss *how are we* going to get this law passed? (Don't let your students get by with this!)

The Exclamation Mark/Point (!)

This mark indicates a strong emotion; it grabs your attention like a pothole and slams on the brakes at the end of an exclamatory sentence.

Ex: If we don't stop, we're going to go over the cliff!

It's also used to indicate a strong interjection, unlike the comma, which introduces a weak interjection.

Ex: Oh no! Are you kidding? No way! I'm jumping out!
Ex: Darn!

IN-BETWEEN MARKS

Readers need more than just end marks in order to appreciate and enjoy the written word. These marks are the little navigators that keep audiences informed and comfortable as they make their way through a piece of writing; they ensure a nice flow, or what we call sentence fluency. Let's start with the comma, the most common road sign. It's also the most underused, overused, misused, and misunderstood, so buckle up!

The Comma (,)

It is used to separate words or phrases in a series:

Ex: Lily finished her *peas, potatoes, and salad*, so her mom let her dive into her dessert.
Ex: Lily ignored her *peas, picked at her potatoes, and spread her salad around her plate*, so her mom did not offer her a dessert.

Note: The Oxford comma—the one before *and* that precedes the final word or phrase in a series—is essential. Without it the reader has to stop to clarify meaning:

Ex: We're having dinner with the Millers, Marty and Marsha. (Are Marty and Marsha a couple named Miller? Are they unrelated individuals? We don't know.)

The comma is also used to connect two independent clauses with one of the seven coordinating conjunctions. The following sentences feature the coordinating conjunctions, but not in alphabetical order. Some teachers have their students repeat them in alphabetical order until they sink in; others have them memorize them with the help of the acronym FANBOYS:

Ex: She gladly helps out with chores, *for* she knows her parents are very busy.

Ex: Serena has a big family, *and* she is the oldest child.
Ex: Serena never forgets the recycling, *nor* does she try to avoid doing the dishes.
Ex: Her status comes with lots of responsibilities, *but* Serena never complains.
Ex: Serena's siblings know they have to follow her lead, *or* else they won't develop good habits.
Ex: This devoted daughter is weary by bedtime, *yet* she takes time to read to her baby sister.
Ex: Serena does get bored at times, *so* she juggles the clean glasses as she puts them away.

Note: When combining two independent clauses, it's often advisable to drop *both* the comma and the subject (or the subject pronoun) from the second clause:

Ex: Every day, Nate walks the dog, and he tutors his brother in math.

This sentence could be streamlined: "Every day, Nate walks the dog and tutors his brother in math."

The comma is also used in the following instances:
To indicate a direct address:

Ex: Lily, please eat your salad.
Ex: Please eat your salad, *Lily*.
Ex: Please, *Lily*, eat your salad.

To introduce a quote:

Ex: Tom asked, "Why are you standing there, Lily?"

To attribute a quote:

Ex: "Why," *Tom asked,* "are you standing there, Lily?" (The comma after *asked* separates the attribution from the rest of the quote, so in this case "Tom asked" also becomes an *interrupter*.

To separate phrases that introduce or end an independent clause:

Ex: Like Simon, I value friends whom I can trust.
Ex: I value friends whom I can trust, *as does Simon*.

To set off *conjunctive adverbs*:

Ex: Lily didn't finish her supper; *consequently,* she was not offered dessert.

To set off *transitional phrases*:

Ex: Lily didn't finish her supper; *as a result,* she was not offered dessert.

Note: There is a list of conjunctive adverbs and transitional phrases in appendix C.

To separate *number periods* (hundreds from thousands, thousands from millions, etc.):

Ex: 999 + 1 = 1,000 (Riddle: When do you use a comma to indicate a period? Only in math.)

To record *dates*:

Ex: On July 4, 2019, Lily will turn 18.

Note: When writing *just* a month and year, *do not* separate them with a comma: In *July 2019*, Lily will turn 18.

To record *addresses*:

Ex: Lily lives at 9901 Greenleaf Avenue, Hollywood, California 90211.

Note: Do not place a comma after a house number or between a state and a zip code.

To set off *interrupters* (nonrestrictive clauses, appositives, and other phrases):

Note: All types of interrupters are set off in commas, and they often hold helpful information, but, to earn their commas, these words or phrases must pass the *nonrestrictive* test—a writer has to ask herself this question: if I take away this phrase, will I change (or *restrict*) the basic meaning of my sentence? If the answer is no, then the phrase is nonrestrictive and needs to be set off in commas. Think of it as an "extra" that is nice to have but not essential. (Reread the first part of this note and leave out "and they often hold helpful information" and "to earn their commas.") Now you see that these phrases *do not* restrict the meaning of the sentence.

Restrictive clauses, then, *do* restrict meaning. Consider this sentence: "Ernest Hemingway's book *For Whom the Bell Tolls* was published in 1940." Because the statement has no commas, it's clear that the writer is referring *only* to Hemingway's 1940 book—not any others—so if the title of the book were removed from the sentence, it would be meaningless. One reason this is hard for kids to understand is that when they see commas around a group of words they think of them as being physically "restricted" by the commas; thus, they get confused.

Nonrestrictive clauses and their restrictive counterparts:

Ex (nonrestrictive): Malik's flute, *that was made 200 years ago,* is very valuable.

Ex (restrictive): Malik's flute *that was made 200 years ago* is very valuable. (He has more than one flute, and the others were *not* made 200 years ago; as a result, they are probably *not* as valuable.)

Ex (nonrestrictive): Electric cars, *which have powerful batteries,* are cheap to operate.

Ex (restrictive): Electric cars *which have powerful batteries* are cheap to operate. (This sentence implies that electric cars vary in terms of battery power.)

To set off appositives (appositives *rename,* or describe in different terms, a noun or pronoun; the word comes from the Latin *apponere* (to put near), so an appositive is *near* in meaning to the noun or pronoun it's renaming):

Ex: Maria's dad, *a dentist,* makes sure his daughter brushes her teeth.
Ex: When Maria gets a toothache, she runs to her dad, *a dentist.*
Ex: Facebook, *a social medium,* has hundreds of millions of users.

Note: Appositives are much like *subject synonyms,* and they represent a skill that young writers desperately need to practice; for example, a student writing about Facebook might repeat that company name several times, when he would do better to mix it up by calling it a "social medium," "corporate giant," or "the company that Mark Zuckerberg started."

To set off other types of phrases:

Ex: Before we ate the dog had to be walked. (There needs to be a comma after ate, of course, which the writer would have known had he read about commas to set off adverbial phrases in chapter 26, "Grammar.")

Before an afterthought (this is like a coda at the end of a movement of a musical composition):

Ex: Bailey chose not to accept the invitation, *a decision she later regretted.*
Ex: Brendan fell back on his bed, *exhausted.*

To set off a weak interjection:

Ex: "*So,* what are you thinking?" asked Lily.
Ex: Oh well, I'll just have to accept it and move on.

To separate two adjectives that modify the same noun (see the discussion of this in chapter 26, "Grammar").

Quotation Marks (" ")

Most often, quotation marks are needed to enclose the words spoken by characters in narrative (including dialogue), or words that have been written or spoken by someone other than the writer. They are also used to identify titles, as well as words or phrases that are not to be taken literally. Here are some examples:

To identify spoken words in dialogue or narrative:

>   *Ex:* Billy turned to the girl sitting next to him and said, *"Excuse me, you're Clara, right?"*
>   *Ex:* *"Yes,"* she replied, *"but why do you ask?"*
>   *Ex:* *"Well,"* Billy began, *"the other day I was asking my friend Evan if you had a boyfriend, and he said, 'Why don't you ask her yourself?'"*
>   *Ex:* *"And?"* she teased.
>   *Ex:* *"And—um—well—do you?"* Billy stammered.
>   *Ex:* *"No,"* Clara replied, *"but now I know why Evan said to me, 'My friend Billy thinks it would be cool if you invited him to see our new high school musical, "Grease"'!"*
>   *Ex:* *"Do you think it would be cool?"*
>   *Ex:* *"Can't you tell? I just did."*

Note: Quotation marks and their placement start to come naturally with practice, but developing writers often place them around *attributions*, and they don't get enough practice punctuating quotes within quotes (as in the example above). Also, as the last two lines above demonstrate, writers can skip attributions when it's obvious who's doing the talking.

To indicate whether all, or only a part of, a sentence is a question or exclamation:

>   *Ex:* "Clara, did Evan really say, 'Clara, you should invite Billy to the play'"? (The question *starts* with "Did" and continues to the end of the sentence, so the question mark goes outside the final quotation marks.) But . . .
>   *Ex:* "No, Billy, but he did say, 'I can't stand musicals!'" (Here, the exclamation *does not* trace back to the person initiating the sentence; it's only expressed by Evan, so the mark, as well as the emotion, are contained within the quotation marks.)

To highlight words that are not to be taken literally:

Ex: Billy picked up his date, Clara, in his vintage *"chariot."*

To enclose book chapters, episodes of ongoing stories, articles, speeches, short stories, short poems, and songs. (As always, the names of books, newspapers, magazines, and other longer works are set in italic type or, if written by hand, underlined.)

Further notes about quotation marks:

- Semicolons, colons, and dashes are *always* placed *outside* quotation marks.
- In America, we still place periods and commas *inside* quotation marks.
- It's okay to place a question mark or exclamation mark outside quotation marks, but *only* if it is punctuating the whole sentence.

- Punctuating long quotes that span *more than one paragraph* is easy: place a period at the end of the first quoted paragraph, indent, and place quotation marks at the beginning of the second paragraph; repeat as needed until the quote is finished.

The Semicolon (;)

The semicolon is like a rolling stop; the period says, "It's the end," but the comma says, "Not so fast; this thought isn't over yet."

It is used to connect two independent clauses when the second one flows naturally from the first:

Ex: I'm sorry I didn't leave you any food; I was starving!

Ex: Mom surprised me with a new bike; I couldn't wait to try it out!

Note: If these clauses were separated by a period, the mood of the moment would deflate.

Sometimes, though, the sense of urgency is not there; the second clause follows on the heels of the first simply because it's closely related:

Ex: Macy's mom didn't believe her; she knew better.

Ex: Hector knows what needs to be done; he just can't seem to do it.

Note: In the two examples immediately above, it would be perfectly acceptable to use a comma and a coordinating conjunction instead of a semicolon: "Macy's mom didn't believe her, *for* she knew better," or, "Hector knows what needs to be done, *but* he just can't seem to do it"—it's just a matter of context, voice, and style. On the other hand, if the semicolons in the first two examples were replaced by commas and coordinating conjunctions, the intended meaning would fall flat.

To introduce conjunctive adverbs:

Ex: Mohammed didn't study for the test; *consequently,* he failed it.

Ex: Your essay is late, Eva; *furthermore,* it lacks a concluding paragraph.

To introduce a transitional phrase:

Ex: Mohammed studied hard for the test; *as a result,* he aced it.

Ex: I didn't say Sheila lacked the skills to do the job; *as a matter of fact,* I think she'd be perfect.

Note: Lists of conjunctive adverbs and transitional phrases can be found in appendix C.

To separate categories that contain internal commas:

Ex: To prepare for our camping trip, we need to pack the camp stove, gas lantern, and pots and pans; plates, knives, forks, spoons, and napkins;

and a dishpan, dish detergent, sponges, and dish towels. (The categories are *cooking*, *eating*, and *cleaning up*.)

Ex: Our family recycles everything: soda cans, aluminum foil, and scrap metal; newspapers, magazines, junk mail, paper bags, and cardboard; glass jars and beverage bottles; and plastics—food containers, grocery bags, and juice bottles. (The categories are *metal, paper, glass,* and *plastic*.)

To set off long independent clauses, or those that have internal commas:

Ex: When she was in high school, Althea sang in the choir, wrote several original vocal pieces, and helped raise money for the choir's out-of-town trips; but she managed to find time to compete on the debate team, build sets for theater productions, and organize a city-park cleanup effort.

Note: It's acceptable to include multiple phrases in a sentence *without* the help of semicolons, but there must be only a few, and they need to be rather short.

Ex: Every night, I drink a glass of milk, wash my face, and brush my teeth before I go to bed.

To separate numbered items (1. bags; 2. forks; 3. spoons, etc.).

Finally, think about giving your students a chance to hone their semicolon skills by writing their own obituary. Yes, it's weird, and it would not be appropriate for the very young, but then they're probably not ready for semicolons anyway.

Textbox 27.1. Student Obituary Lesson

WHAT YOU NEED TO KNOW

- While this exercise focuses on the use of semicolons to separate groups of people (the deceased's survivors), it also gives kids a chance to create a "fantasy" past for themselves.
- These obituaries should be rather short—perhaps three hundred words—and include a work history of the deceased; other interests and activities; a list of surviving relatives, as well as those who preceded him or her in death; information about a funeral or celebration of life; and details about where to send memorials (the deceased's favorite charity, medical research organizations, etc.).

WHAT YOU NEED TO DO

- Show your students some examples of obituaries—the skinny ones printed in the local newspaper—and point out how semicolons are used to organize the deceased's family.
- Tell your students to have fun creating a long life, a big family, tremendous jobs, and exciting and worthwhile pastimes!

The Apostrophe (')

Here are the ways to use an apostrophe:
   To make contractions:

Ex: do not = *don't*

To indicate omitted letters or numbers:

Ex: Heather was born in *'95.*
Ex: He's always *singin'* in the rain.

To form plurals:

Ex: For easy understanding, the plurals of lowercase letters require apostrophes: mind your *p's* and *q's.* However, uppercase letters, numerals, and acronyms do not need apostrophes for clarity: *Ss, 3s* (threes), *20s* (twenties), *EMTs* (Emergency Medical Technicians).

To indicate singular possession:

Ex: Andrea's dog is very cute.
Ex: Gus's dog is cute too.
Ex: Marlys's dog is not cute at all!

To indicate plural possession (group ownership):

Ex: John and Mary Adams have three children; all of the Adamses live together in a big house.
Ex: The *Adamses'* dog lives in his own house, outside.
Ex: Their *children's* cats live in the house, but the *neighbors'* cats run wild. (multiple neighbors)
Ex: The Adamses don't want other *people's* cats interacting with theirs.

Note: Some young writers have the habit of placing apostrophes on the pronouns *theirs, ours,* and *yours,* as well as the possessive form of it: *its.*
   To indicate possession that's shared:

Ex: We've been invited to *John and Mary's* house for dinner.

Ex: Nathan, Josh, Sarah, and Jack's band is playing tonight. (The apostrophe and the *s* are added *only* to the name of the last owner, no matter how many there are.)

To show possession with compound nouns:

Ex: Her *father-in-law's* cabin was a fun family gathering place. (She has one father-in-law.)

Ex: The *fathers-in-law's* club holds a meeting every year. (There are several fathers-in-law.)

Ex: The *attorney general's* staff joined her for the press conference. (One attorney general.)

Ex: All of the states' *attorneys general's* suggestions were welcomed by the president. (Several state attorneys general met with the president.)

To show possession with indefinite pronouns:

Ex: Everyone's opinion is valued here.

Ex: Let's get *someone else's* opinion now, shall we?

To show possession with an adjective:

Ex: Yesterday's storm was scary. (*Yesterday* is the adjective here.)

Ex: This *week's* weather looks pretty good. (*Week* is an adjective here.)

Two notes regarding possessive apostrophes:

While many believe that there is no need, when indicating possession by tacking an apostrophe onto the end of a noun that ends in *s*, to follow it with an extra *s*, this author does not. This practice poses no problems for readers, but it does for listeners: when members of the broadcast media refer to something that someone owns, for example, they almost *never* pronounce the possessive *s* that's necessary to let listeners know the name of the owner.

Ex: Let's say pitcher Freddie Mays's elbow is acting up, so he's benched. If the sports reporter covering the story doesn't pronounce the extra *s*, the audience won't know if his name is Mays or May.

Possessive apostrophes confuse all of us at times, but a simple suggestion often helps: Write (or project) examples of the various possessive apostrophe situations outlined above, and demonstrate for your students how to draw a line under the noun in question, stopping *at the end* of it. Now, draw a vertical arrow upward, which will point to the spot that the apostrophe should land. (Sometimes it's not enough to simply say, "Students, just remember to place the apostrophe after the owner.")

The Ellipsis (...)

To indicate that *thought* is interrupting speech:

Ex: "Well, Mom, I . . . ah . . . can't really tell you . . . ah . . . what happened."

To indicate that (unnecessary) words have been deleted from a quotation:

Ex: In his address to his employees, the CEO said, "We've come a long way here at Doggie Digital, and I thank you . . . next week's rollout of our new GPS collar will revolutionize the industry . . . the virtual goggles are still in development . . . eventually, we will succeed in our secret research into canine-to-human telepathy!"

The Hyphen (-)

The need to divide a word at the end of a line of type has been eliminated by the word processor, but, for those who still use a typewriter or a pencil, here are some pointers: Divide words *only* between syllables; don't divide one-syllable words (stretch) or short words (apple); don't create a one-syllable "orphan" (i-solate).

When writing fractions, use hyphens between the numerator and denominator: one-fourth (1/4). If the numerators or denominators, themselves, need to be hyphenated, *do not* place yet another hyphen between them: *eight thirty-seconds* (8/32) or *twenty-one thirty-seconds* (21/32)—*not* eight-thirty-seconds or twenty-one-thirty-seconds.

Hyphenate *two-word* numbers, starting with twenty-one and ending with ninety-nine. Beyond that, write *one hundred . . . one hundred one . . . one hundred twenty . . . one hundred twenty-one*, etc.

Hyphens are used to make compound words: out-of-town guests, built-in dishwasher.

Similarly, they connect capital letters with other words, often to create adjectives: T-shirt, X-ray, A-rated company.

Hyphens also sit between prefixes and suffixes to help describe nouns or actions:

Ex: I only eat *gluten-free* food.
Ex: This is a *self-cleaning* oven.
Ex: The *ex-Marine* visited our school.
Ex: In order to switch to a different resort, we had to *re-sort* our belongings for the move.

Finally, hyphens have been very kind to us readers; they've made the task of sorting out meaning a lot less frustrating. Nowadays, however, they're beginning to disappear:

Ex: She's the *preeminent* expert. (not pre-eminent)
Ex: Let's *rerecord* the song. (not re-record)
Ex: Next year we will *reelect* our mayor. (not re-elect)

Ex: It was a *yearlong* effort to get the bill passed. (not year-long)

For now, though, *reallife*, *shellike*, and *falllike* are still out of bounds; time will tell.

The Dash (—)

This mark is "dashing" to the head of the punctuation standings, probably because it reflects our frenetic behavior. Its uses:

To indicate interrupted speech:

> *Ex:* "Hi—no, that's okay—what?—well, I guess, but—huh?—sure, I'll wait for your call back."

To interrupt the smooth flow of a sentence in order to provide information that just can't wait to be expressed in a proper sentence of its own:

> *Ex:* Tom told me something—I can't remember what it was at the moment—about your plan. It might have had to do with cost—yes, that was it—and it's causing me to doubt the integrity of the whole project.

A dash can also be used for emphasis, which is related to both the above use and one of the uses of the colon (below).

> *Ex:* Principal Peters has one major goal for the year—improved test scores.
>
> *Ex:* If you can turn three things around this year, Derek—attendance, behavior, and attentiveness—you will finish the year in good shape.

The Colon (:)

This mark could be called the "double period"; the first signals a complete stop, and the second tells us to stay there and think about what might be waiting up ahead. Its uses:

To emphasize something:

> *Ex:* The greatest threat to humanity might be one of the tiniest beings on earth: bacteria.

To introduce a statement or quotation:

> *Ex:* My father gave me some very good advice: listen most closely to yourself.
>
> *Ex:* President Kennedy aroused our sense of patriotism with this appeal: "Ask not what your country can do for you—ask what you can do for your country."

To introduce a list:

Ex: Be sure to bring the following items: binoculars, a notebook, a pencil, and a water bottle.

Note: It's important to teach students *not* to launch into a list by introducing it with a verb ("Be sure to *bring*: binoculars, a notebook . . ."), but with what's called a *summary word* (like "items" in the above example). Colons indicate a solid break, but verbs indicate continuing motion; therefore, a verb serves to introduce the list all by itself, without the need for a colon. (Gerunds, however, are possible exceptions to this rule: "He's got a lot going: homework, sports, choir, . . .")

After the salutation in a business letter:

Ex: To whom it may concern:
Ex: Dear Chairman Smith:

Between numerals indicating hours, minutes, and seconds:

Ex: We'll start the meeting at *8:00* a.m. sharp.
Ex: Mark's time for the race was one hour, three minutes, and forty-five seconds (*01:03:45*).

To express ratios:

Ex: Two parts water to one part rice is a *2:1* ratio.

To represent analogies:

Ex: Good is to bad as happy is to sad can also be expressed *good : bad :: happy : sad*.

Parentheses ( )

These are used to surround information that's dropped into a sentence:

Ex: The man is amazing; he can build anything *(birdhouses, dog houses, people houses, etc.)*, and he still has time to spare!

Note: Punctuation within parentheses only applies to the parenthetical content; punctuation that exists outside the parentheses applies to the sentence as a whole.

Chapter Twenty-Eight

Spelling

Many people today (including some teachers) ask the question, "Why do students need to learn spelling when they have spell-check to bail them out?" The simplest answer is that it's educational: words have histories that hold secrets about other, related, words, and we can unlock them by examining their roots—it all starts with sounds and letters.

When children are very young, they begin learning the English phonemes (the sounds that letters and their combinations make), as well as their written counterparts (phonograms). They point at letters and attempt to "read." When they get to school, they start hearing the sounds and seeing the letter combinations everywhere. It's like that strange phenomenon that occurs right after you buy a car that you thought was pretty unique, and suddenly you see them all over town! Youngsters, then, actually start learning *phonics* before they enter school.

Sadly, though, as they begin their formal training, few of them are exposed to a curriculum that picks up where they left off. Students should learn *all* of the phonograms and study spelling words that are aligned with them, but what passes for spelling instruction today is often rote memorization of word lists that have no structural theme. Why?

A few decades ago, teachers began hearing the phrase "invented spelling," which, when coupled with the then-popular notion that *phonics* is a dirty word, gave them tacit approval to cease teaching spelling at all. It's ironic, for there is nothing inherently wrong with invented spelling; after all, preschoolers, who *naturally* study phonics, are charter subscribers. But teachers need to take them to the next level by providing formal, phonics-based spelling curricula. This chapter aims to help return spelling to its rightful place as the crucial third leg of the reading and writing triad.

Chapter 28

WHAT YOU NEED TO KNOW

- This chapter is *not* an instructional guide to teaching spelling. Its purpose is to convince teachers that spelling is important, introduce them to the sounds that letter combinations make, highlight the most important rules of spelling, and provide them with many themed lists.
- The practicality of being able to quickly tap out the correct letters on a keyboard outshouts the more-important reasons to study spelling: it teaches us to read faster, it improves our comprehension, and it produces a web of related words to add to one's vocabulary.
- Etymology must play a role in any spelling program. The study of word origins reveals why words mean what they do, and it opens our eyes to their modern relatives that surround us—suddenly we understand how they came about. Think about teaching how to tell time on an analogue clock: we look to astronomy for an explanation, which, in turn, allows our students to visualize the connection between the rotation of the earth and the turning of the hands on a clock. The point? Our friend spell-check teaches us as much about words as a digital clock teaches us about astronomy—that is to say, not much.
- Themed lists are an important component of a truly meaningful spelling curriculum; they reveal characteristics that many words have in common—lending purpose to their study—and they turn what can otherwise be a boring exercise into a valuable (and fun) learning experience.

WHAT YOU NEED TO DO

- Check out www.spalding.org. This organization (Spalding Education International) is the go-to source for teachers who are serious about spelling instruction. They offer courses to all public, private, and charter schools, as well as to individual teachers; they even have an online course for home educators.
- Look at the sample lists in figures 28.1 and 28.2 to get an idea of the spelling-related resources available in this book. The first eight lists feature some of the phonograms that are an integral part of the Spalding program, and the rest are author-developed, themed lists.
- Mind the rules! The bad news is that there are about thirty of them; the good news is that most of them, while not less important than the others, are a bit less critical. (Sign up for Spalding training if you want to learn them all!)

Spelling List Sampler

A Sounds (as in 'blame')

a e	ea	ei	ai	ay	ey	eigh
bare	bear	beige	faint	clay	prey	eight

Aw Sounds (as in 'saw')

aw	au	ough	augh
claw	fault	bought	naughty

Er Sounds (Bert's bird burps worms early)

er	ir	ur	wor	ear
fertile	thirst	turkey	worry	heard

E Sounds (as in 'Pete')

ē	e e	ee	ea	ie	ei	ey
recipe	mere	steel	steal	field	seize	monkey

O Sounds (as in 'tote')

o e	ou	oe	oa	ough	ow	oo
snore	your	floe	gloat	although	tomorrow	floor

I Sounds (as in 'site')

ī	ī e	y	ei	igh
icon	kite	sty	height	sigh

Ow Sounds (as in 'cloud')

ou	ough	ow
cloud	drought	chowder

Sh, zh Sounds (as in partial, division)

sh	sh	sh	zh
martial	delicious	fission	vision

Figure 28.1.

For now, here are four rules that your students need to be aware of, and that apply broadly:

(1) The familiar *i* before *e*, except after *c*, or when sounded like *a* as in *neighbor* and *weigh*. (*Note: eigh* is known as the "four-letter *a*" in the Spalding method.) The *exceptions* to this rule can be memorized by learning a couple of silly phrases. The first one was coined by Romalda Spalding, the originator of the Spalding method; the second is the author's take on other exceptions noted by Spalding:

Silent Letters

b	c	g	h	k
comb	indict, scent	gnome, sign	rhubarb	know

p	s	t	w
receipt	aisle	listen	wrap

Groups of Confusing Spellings

coral	corral	chorale	choral	carol	carrel
paddle	pedal	peddle	petal	piddle	puddle
peer	pier	pure	pear	pare	pair

Words Ending in 'l', not 'le'

annual	anvil	aural	Babel	basil	bevel	bezel

Latin and Greek Roots

Root	Origin	Meaning	Examples
aero-	Greek	air	aeroplane, aerial, aerobic, aerosol
astro-	Greek	star	asterisk, astronomer, asteroid, aster
aud-	Latin	hear	audition, auditory, auditorium, audible, aural
avi-	Latin	bird	aviary, aviation

Mispronounced, thus Misspelled Words

realtor ('relator')	sherbet ('sherbert')	recognize ('reconnize')	strength ('strenth')	picture ('pitcher')

Figure 28.2.

    a. *Neither foreign sovereign seized the counterfeit and forfeited leisure.* (In each of these words, *i* is not before *e*, there's no *c* involved, and there's no long *a* sound, so the rule doesn't hold.)

    b. *Either weird heifer gives protein.* (Here, again, *i* is not before *e*, there's no *c* in sight, and there's no long *a* sound, so the rule doesn't hold.)

Note: There are other exceptions to this rule, such as *sleight* and the name *Keith*.

(2) Spalding's Rule 10, reworded: Imagine a two-syllable word (*commit*) that ends in a consonant (*t*) that's preceded by a vowel (*i*). Now, let's say you want to change the word by adding *-ing* or *-ed*. Do you double the *t* or not? It's easy—just notice if the accent is on the first syllable of the word

(*com*•mit) or on the second (com•*mit*). Obviously, the first option sounds ridiculous, so if the accent is on the first syllable, *do not* double the *t*; if it's on the second, *do* double the *t*.

Examples:

wor•ship, so . . . *wor*•ship•ing
col•or, so . . . *col*•or•ing
ad•*mit*, so . . . ad•*mit*•ted
re•*fer*, so . . . re•*fer*•ring

Note: Spalding goes on to say that the British don't pay as much attention to this rule as Americans do. This author heartily agrees and advises students to follow the rule strictly, for doing so will never be deemed incorrect; breaking it might—even in Britain.

(3) The five silent final *e*'s (featured in Spalding under Rule 7):

a. The *e* at the end of a word makes the vowel say its own name. *Ex:* late, here, bite, hope, cute.
b. English words do not end in *v* or the *single* vowel *u*, so we add an *e*. *Ex:* have, dove, value, clue (*menu* and *ecru* are rare exceptions).
c. Silent *e* is added to words ending in *c* or *g* so that they end in a "soft" sound. *Ex: Brace* without the *e* would sound like "brack," and *barge* would sound like "barg."
d. Since English words must contain a vowel in every syllable, we add an *e*. *Ex: Bicycle* would still say "bi•cy•cl" without the *e*, but then it would lack a vowel in the third syllable, and that's a no-no. (There are lots of other words that have two consonants in a row in their final syllables—*fiddle*, *able*, *simple*, *wiggle*, *sprinkle*, *puzzle*, *waffle*, *hassle*, and *whittle*, to name a few.)
e. The (Spalding) "no-job *e*" is everyone's favorite, even though, as its name suggests, it's useless. And, while one could question the value of rules (b) and (d), this final *e* seems especially unnecessary. For one reason or another, however, many such words have survived their etymological journeys. *Ex:* mouse, come, purpose, have, valve, troupe, impulse, horse.

Note: This author's name surely ended in *e* at some point in the past, but he has not missed it.

(4) There are five ways to say *er* in English. This is called Rule 8 in the Spalding method, and it's modeled there as follows: H*er* f*ir*st n*ur*se w*or*ks *ear*ly. Because so many words contain the *er* sound, it's imperative that young spellers learn to match them with the correct phonograms. Point out to your students, though, that *or* almost always says *er* if it's preceded by *w* (*worn* is an exception) and that *ear* often does *not* say *er* (*tear*, *heart*).

Section IV

Appendixes

Almost all the materials in these appendixes are available for download on the *Keys to Inspiration* book page at https://rowman.com/ISBN/9781475838725/Keys-to-Inspiration-A-Teacher's-Guide-to-a-Student-Centered-Writing-Program. Go there and click on the Features tab, which will take you to the online documents.

Appendix A

Spelling Lists

LONG *A* (A_E, EA, AI, EI, AY, EY, EIGH)

bare	bear
beige	faint
clay	prey
eight	grate
feign	feint
survey	gait
gate	slate
slay	neigh
break	surveillance
vein	reindeer
campaign	obey
freight	complain
pare	pale
rain	pear
rein	reign
whale	restrain
sleigh	payday

strait straight
pray neighbor
shape

AW AS IN SAW (AW, AU, OUGH, AUGH)

claw fault
bought naughty
sought fawn
taut taunt
taught cause
thought thaw
haughty flaws
applause daunting
fraught maul
maw brought
fought haunt
awning cough
ought trough
shawl yawn
brawn autumn
crawl bawl
caught withdrawal
daughter laud
nautical gnaw
plausible lawyer

ER (BERT'S BIRD BURPS WORMS EARLY; ER, IR, UR, WOR, EAR)

fertile thirst
turkey worry
heard shepherd
circle sturdy

world	earnest
perky	stirring
further	worst
dearth	vertical
girdle	urn
worship	earth
work	berm
worm	verge
merge	clergy
alert	dessert
squirt	flirt
twirl	splurge
disturb	purpose
furrow	curb
twirl	concern
desert	squirm

LONG E (Ē, E_E, EE, EA, IE, EI, EY)

recipe	steel
steal	field
seize	mere
mete	fleece
beat	yield
either	journey
eke	career
creature	niece
ceiling	money
streak	shield
appeal	beetle
believe	beneath
calliope	leisure
monkey	ether

bleed	protein
neither	weird
sneeze	wield
year	tier
tear	feature
peace	piece

LONG O (Ō, O_E, OU, OE, OA, OUGH, OW, OO)

snore	your
floe	gloat
although	tomorrow
floor	mote
pour	mistletoe
piccolo	thorough
shadow	door
clone	four
flown	moat
dough	harrow
below	board
borough	borrow
burrow	coarse
grown	minnow
oboe	roast
row	roe
soar	solo
croak	follow
hoe	chore
though	toast

LONG I (Ī, I_E, Y, EI, IGH)

icon	sty

height
cacti
slight
fungi
imply
fright
rabbi
confine
sign
sarcophagi
alibi
die
fiber
high
kite
site
quite
right
nuclei

sigh
sleight
might
horrify
satisfy
cite
stein
benign
tie-dye
flight
cyanide
octopi
Geiger counter
gigantic
nylon
plight
rye
resign
rite

OW AS IN CLOUD (OU, OUGH, OW)

cloud
chowder
shroud
scout
bowsprit
scow
ground
flower
slouch
vowel
flour

drought
cowboy
clown
bough
sprout
tower
trout
shower
spouse
ouch
jowl

meow
plough
about
counter
gadabout
announcement
downside
coward
bower

plowshare
boundary
pound
espouse
countenance
bountiful
downspout
drought
trowel

SH AND ZH WORDS

martial
vision
excruciating
fusion
ocean
substantial
regime
seizure
marshal
equation
electrician
passion
beige
lesion
casual
confusion
musician
financial
initial
unusual

delicious
fission
official
mission
pleasure
special
facial
officious
precious
crucial
permission
tension
torsion
judicial
logician
magician
provincial
omniscient
demolition
version

Appendix B

Spelling-Related Lists

SILENT LETTERS

comb	indict	exhibit
gnome	rhubarb	knee
scissors	wrist	raspberry
fascinated	salmon	knuckle
scent	plumber	rhinoceros
moisten	thistle	aghast
gnu	tomb	knot
wrangle	Arkansas	wrought
knack	knoll	mortgage
numb	dumb	coup
silhouette	honest	rhetoric
scenic	limb	psychic
island	Christmas	know
receipt	aisle	science
listen	wrap	hasten
gnash	cupboard	knit
gnat	lamb	rhyme

180   *Appendix B*

wreck	knock	pneumatic
whistle	muscle	hour
psychiatrist	mnemonic	gneiss
Champagne	honor	foreign
ghetto	apostle	exhaust
vehicle	pseudonym	campaign
feign	wrong	sword
ghost	Rhode Island	pneumonia
knob	solder	benign
crumb	exhort	corps
ghoul	descend	glisten
resign	exhilarating	vehement
sovereign	rapport	thumb
climb	debt	fasten
reign	gherkin	Connecticut
vogue	Illinois	wrestle
gnaw	gnarly	ghastly
plumb	knight	wright
psalm	debut	ascent
knapsack	wring	rhythm
doubt	wrinkle	sign
align	soften	

GROUPS OF CONFUSING SPELLINGS

aisle	modal
I'll	model
isle	mottle
allusion	moral
illusion	morel
away	Moro

aweigh	morro
	morrow
bazaar	marrow
bizarre	
	muscle
borrow	mussel
barrow	
barrel	paddle
beryl	pedal
borough	peddle
burrow	petal
burro	piddle
	puddle
canvas	
canvass	peer
	pier
collared	pure
collard	pear
colored	pair
	pare
college	
collage	pore
colleague	pour
collegial	poor
coral	pistil
corral	pistol
chorale	
choral	pommel
carol	pummel
carrel	
	plaintiff

carrot
caret
karat

demure
demur

desperate
disparate
despair

discomfit
discomfort

fascia
facial
fascist
fashion
fuchsia

feign
faint
feint
fake

gauge
gouge
gauche
gouache

heroine
heroin

plaintive

principal
principle

rain
reign
rein

rappel
repel
repeal

regimen
regiment
regime

relieve
relive
relevé

revere
revel
reveille
revile
reveal

suppose
supposed
supposedly
supposable
supposably

mantel
mantle
mental
medal
meddle
metal
mettle

missal
missile
mistletoe

vial
vile
viral

with
wither
whither
withers
withering
whether
weather

WORDS ENDING IN *L*

annual
aural
basil
bezel
brothel
cabal
carol
choral
cymbal
doggerel
equal
familial
fennel
final
floral
fossil
funeral
funnel

anvil
Babel
bevel
boreal
bushel
cancel
carrel
coral
Cyril
easel
facial
fecal
feral
finial
focal
frugal
fungal
furl

gimbals	global
gravel	Gretel
grovel	gunnel
Handel	hazel
hospital	hovel
idol	infidel
isle	jackal
kennel	kernel
label	laurel
lentil	level
lintel	literal
marvel	mantel
medieval	medal
metal	mental
modal	missal
mogul	model
moral	mongrel
mortal	morsel
mussel	mural
naval	nasal
newel	navel
nominal	nickel
nostril	normal
official	novel
oral	opal
oval	oriel
Papal	panel
pedal	passel
perpetual	pedestal
pistil	petal
pivotal	pistol
portal	pommel

principal	primal
quarrel	pummel
reciprocal	rascal
sandal	rival
scandal	satchel
shovel	scoundrel
sisal	shrivel
sorrel	snorkel
spiral	special
symbol	squirrel
tidal	tassel
travel	trammel
twirl	tunnel
viral	vial
vital	vocal
weasel	whirl
whorl	

RULE 10 WORDS

Spalding's Rule 10 pertains to two-syllable words that end in a consonant preceded by a vowel. If the root word is accented on the first syllable, do not double the final consonant before adding endings such as *–ed* and *–ing*. If the accent is on the second syllable, double the consonant.

If the accent is on the first syllable, do not double the consonant.

alter	harbor	open
badger	harrow	order
border	label	panel
borrow	layer	pedal
burrow	limit	signal
cancel	litter	travel
clamor	major	vomit
color	marvel	wander

cover	mentor	water
edit	model	wonder
factor	mother	worship
flatter	motor	
hammer	murder	

If the accent is on the second syllable, double the consonant.

abet	control	rappel
abhor	corral	rebel
acquit	defer	recur
admit	demur	refer
allot	deter	refit
befit	excel	regret
begin	incur	remit
combat	occur	repel
commit	omit	repot
concur	permit	submit
confer	prefer	

LATIN AND GREEK ROOTS

Root	Origin	Meaning	Examples
aero-	Greek	air	aeroplane, aerial, aerobic, aerosol
astro-	Greek	star	asterisk, astronomer, asteroid, aster
aud-	Latin	hear	audition, auditory, auditorium, audible, aural
avi-	Latin	bird	aviary, aviation
belli-	Latin	war	belligerent, antebellum, bellicose
bio-	Greek	life	biography, biology, biome

Appendix B

Root	Origin	Meaning	Examples
cap-	Latin	head	capital, captain, chief, decapitate
chrono-	Greek	time	anachronism, chronology, chronicle, asynchronous, chronic
circ-	Latin	around	circumnavigate, circumference, circumcision
cogn-	Latin	recognize	incognito, cognition, cognate
dict-	Latin	speak	diction, dictate, dictionary, contradict
dorm-	Latin	sleep	dormitory, dormant
fac-, -fec, -fic	Latin	make, do	manufacture, benefactor, efficient, facilitate, facsimile, prolific, perfect, qualification
fide-	Latin	trust	fidelity, confide, fiduciary, faith
fin-	Latin	end	finite, infinity, finish
gen-	Greek	birth, type	genome, generation, genealogy, genetic, generator, genesis, genocide, generic, congenital
gen-	Latin	beget	genuine, congenial, genius, indigenous
grad-, gress-	Latin	step, go	gradation, gradual, progress, digression
graph-	Greek	write	graphic, telegraph, phonograph, graphite
hydra-	Greek	water, liquid	hydrate, hydroponics, hydraulic
liber-	Latin	free	liberate, liberal, libertine

Appendix B

Root	Origin	Meaning	Examples
mort-	Latin	death	mortician, mortal, immortal
pan-	Greek	all	panacea, pandemic, panorama, pantheism
pen-	Latin	almost	peninsula, penultimate, penumbra
pen-, pun-	Latin	punish	penalty, penitentiary, penal, impunity, punishment, repent, subpoena
phil-	Greek	love	philanthropy, bibliophile, philharmonic, philosophy
phon-	Greek	sound	phonograph, telephone, phonics, phonetics, cacophony, symphony, microphone
pot-	Latin	power	despot, impotent, possess, potent, potentate, potential, power
quer-, quir-	Latin	search, seek	inquire, query, question, inquest, acquisition, conquest, acquire
rect-	Latin	straight	correct, rectitude, direct, erect, rectum
sci-	Latin	know	science, conscience, subconscious, conscientious, prescient, omniscient, nescient
scrib-, script	Latin	write	scribble, transcribe, subscription, describe, manuscript, scripture, script

Root	Origin	Meaning	Examples
serv-	Latin	save, protect	conserve, deserve, observe, preserve, reserve, servant, service, servile, servitude, subservient
spec-	Latin	look	speculate, spectrum, inspect, respect, aspect, spectator
tele-	Greek	end, far	telegram, telegraph, telemetry, telepathy, television, telephone, telescope
therm-	Greek	heat	thermal, thermometer, hypothermia, thermodynamic, thermostat
trans-	Latin	through	intransigent, transact, transcend, transient, transitory, transparent, transport, translation
vin-	Latin	wine	vinaigrette, vine, vinegar, viniculture
vinc-, vict-	Latin	conquer	convict, conviction, convince, evict, invincible, province, victor, victorious, victory
vit-	Latin	life	vital, vitality, vitamin

MISPRONOUNCED, THUS MISSPELLED, WORDS

Correct Spelling	Mispronunciation and/or Misspelling	Correct Spelling	Mispronunciation and/or Misspelling
affidavit	*affidavid*	anticlimactic	*anticlimatic*
asterisk(s)	*asterix/asteriks*	athlete	*athalete*
bazaar	*bizarre*	bizarre	*bazaar*

Correct Spelling	Mispronunciation and/or Misspelling	Correct Spelling	Mispronunciation and/or Misspelling
biceps	*bicepts*	comfortable	*comfterble*
could have, should have, would have	*could of, should of, would of*	cowlick	*colic*
different	*differnt*	disgust	*discust*
drowned	*drownded*	environment	*envirement*
et cetera	*ek cetera*	February	*Febuary*
government	*goverment*	isthmus	*ithsmus*
jewelry	*jewlery*	nuclear	*nuculer*
ophthalmology	*opthamology*	picture	*pitcher*
realtor	*relator*	probably	*probly*
recognize	*reconnize*	restaurateur	*restranteur*
sacrilegious	*sacreligious*	since	*sense*
sherbet	*sherbert*	strength	*strenth*
suffrage	*sufferage*	supposed	*sposed*
supposedly	*supposably*	temperament	*temperment*
used to	*use to*	Valentine's Day	*Valentime's Day*
verbiage	*verbage*	veterinarian	*vetranarian*
Wednesday	*Wensday*	whether	*wether*
which	*wich*	you're	*your*

CURIOUS SPELLING CHANGES FROM ONE WORD FORM TO ANOTHER

abound, but abundance
absorb, but absorption
abstain, but abstention, abstinence
acclaim, but acclamation
animus, but animosity
anxious, but anxiety
appeal, but appellate
cocoa (the powder), but cacao (the seed from which it's made)
conceive, but conception
consume, but consumption
curious, but curiosity
deceive, but deception
denounce, but denunciation
describe, but description

doubt, but dubious
eat, but edible
enounce, but enunciation
equal; equality, but equity, equilibrium, equivalent, equidistant
exclaim, but exclamation, exclamatory
explain, but explanation
fire, but fiery
four; fourteen, but forty
governor, but gubernatorial
grain, but granular, granola, granary
grateful, but gratitude
heir, but inherit
high, but height
luminous, but luminosity
maintain, but maintenance
memory, but memento
monster, but monstrous, monstrosity
omit, but omission
pertain, but pertinent, impertinence
porous, but porosity
practice, but practitioner
proceed, but procession
proclaim, but proclamation
pronounce, but pronunciation
receive, but reception, receipt
redeem, but redemption
refrigerator, but "fridge"
remain, but remnant
remember, but remembrance
repair, but reparable, irreparable, reparation
repeat, but repetition
restaurant, but restaurateur
reveal, but revelation, revelatory
sheep, but shepherd
speak, but speech
strain, but strenuous
strong, but strength
sustain, but sustenance
thorax, but thoracic
vain, but vanity
vertex, but vertices
viscous, but viscosity
wonder, but wondrous

Appendix C

Other Lists

CONJUNCTIVE ADVERBS AND TRANSITIONAL PHRASES

Conjunctive Adverbs
Edward was very tired; consequently, he couldn't finish his homework.

Transitional Phrases
Sheila was disappointed that it was raining; on the other hand, she realized that the garden needed water.

Conjunctive Adverbs	Transitional Phrases
besides	above all
consequently	after all
conversely	all in all
furthermore	as a matter of fact
however	as a result
indeed	at the same time
instead	by and large
lastly	by this time
likewise	for example
meanwhile	for instance
moreover	in addition
nevertheless	in any event
obviously	in contrast
otherwise	in effect
rather	in either case
regardless	in fact

significantly	in other words
similarly	in particular
still	in summary
surprisingly	in the first place
therefore	in the long run
thus	on the other hand

EMOTIONAL EVENTS

- Loss of a parent, sibling, grandparent, friend, cousin, neighbor, teacher, pet
- Moving to another city, state, or neighborhood
- Parent starting a new job
- Moving to a new house
- Moving to a new school
- Experiencing something new, maybe in another city, state, or country
- Separation or divorce of parents
- Seeing a baby brother or sister for the first time
- Having a new baby in the house
- Having a new pet in the house
- Attending a funeral or visiting someone who is about to die
- First date
- Breaking up
- A serious disagreement or fight with a friend
- Experiencing peer pressure to do something you know is wrong
- Being the victim of a bully or feeling threatened
- A good friend moves away
- A new neighbor becomes a friend
- Realizing someone is not as fortunate as you
- Fire
- Tornado
- Car accident
- Burglary or theft of something dear to you
- It's the big game and you do something great, or not so great
- Music, dance, or theater performance (or another type of performance or competition)
- Witnessing something really cool, maybe rare
- Helping someone who is in trouble
- Emotional or physical abuse
- First times: Diving off the high dive, downhill skiing, riding a bike, airplane ride, looking through a powerful telescope, attending a summer

camp, waterskiing, seeing the northern lights, riding a horse, catching a fish, cooking something special

EMOTIONS AND EMOTION-RELATED WORDS

Nouns

anger	loneliness
anxiety (worry)	longing
bitterness	loss
compassion	love
depression	malaise
desolation	melancholy
elation	nervousness
embarrassment	pain
empathy	panic
emptiness	passion
envy	pity
excitement	pride
exhilaration	regret
fear	rejection
gratitude	relief
grief	resentment
guilt	sadness
happiness	satisfaction
hate	self-consciousness
helplessness	self-pity
homesickness	shame
hope	shock
hopelessness	sorrow
horror	sympathy
hurt	terror
insecurity	thankfulness
intimidation	uneasiness

jealousy
joy

worthlessness
yearning

Verbs

accept
admire
affirm
annoy
appreciate
apologize
belittle
betray
bully
comfort
commiserate
compliment

forgive
harass
humiliate
include
injure
insult
neglect
ostracize
reassure
tease
threaten
tolerate

FACIAL EXPRESSIONS

alert
anguished
anxious
bedazzled
bedraggled
bemused
bewildered
cold
confused
content
contrite
defeated
deflated
delighted

giddy
grim
happy
haughty
helpless
hopeless
horrified
icy
languid
lost
mournful
peaceful
perplexed
placid

desperate
despondent
devilish
disbelieving
drowsy
eager
ecstatic
embarrassed
empty
expectant
forlorn
frightened

radiant
sad
scared
shocked
smug
surprised
suspicious
terrorized
tired
vacant
weary
worried

FACIAL FEATURES, HANDS

Eyes Can Appear...

bright
clear
cold
dead
disarming
distant
dreamy
frightened
happy
hollow
innocent
intoxicating
inviting

laughing
loving
piercing
receptive
revealing
shadowy
smiling
soft
sparkling
starry
sunken
transparent
vacant

Faces Can Appear...

creviced

pleasant

ghostly
hard
long
moon-like

sharp
soft
sullen
weathered

Noses Can Be...

a bill
beaked
bulbous

pointy
pugged
roman

Complexion Can Be...

alabaster
blue-black
chocolate
coffee-with-cream

milky-white
olive
pale
ruddy

Hands/Fingers Can Appear...

bony
calloused
cracked
crepe-paper-like
crooked
delicate
dirty
dry
expensive
experienced
filthy
gnarly
greasy
gritty
groping

manicured
nimble
old
probing
pudgy
rough
scarred
slender
sensitive
soft
smooth
tender
strong
thin
thick

innocent
liver-spotted

young
weathered

HOMOGRAPHS

affect
axes
bases
bass
bow
bower
brat
buffet
close
closer
combine
commune
compact
concert
conduct
console
content
contract
converse
defect
deliberate
desert
digest
does
dove
drawer
entrance
fascia

impact
intern
intimate
invalid
lather
lead
lower
lupine
moderate
mow
number
object
peaked
process
present
project
proceeds
recreate
putting
row
sewer
slaver
sow
subject
tear
viola
wind
wound

IDIOMS, SAYINGS, EXPRESSIONS

Idiom, Saying, Expression	Meaning
She doesn't *have a clue*	She has no idea what this is all about.
It's a bit *over my head*	I don't understand.
Beats me!	I don't know.
That is a *bottom-up* organization	The bosses get input from the workers.
top-down	The opposite of *bottom-up*
hit *rock bottom*	When things can't get any worse for someone, he has hit *rock bottom*.
What's the *bottom line*?	What is the final result; what does it mean?
Where do we *sit*?	What is our current situation? What is our position on this issue?
What's your *pleasure*?	What would you like? What can I get for you?
heart-to-heart	an honest talk with someone about serious matters
You *hit the nail on the head*	You understand. You are absolutely right.
Hit the road!	Get out of here! Leave!
hit the books	To *hit the books* means to study, as you would for a test.
She got a *slap on the wrist*	She received a minor punishment or warning after doing something wrong.
a fish out of water	someone who doesn't know what to do because he is in an unfamiliar situation
on the take	If someone is *on the take*, he is being bribed.
on the mend	recovering from an illness or injury
on the fence	Someone who is *on the fence* can't decide what to do, or which side of an issue to take.
over the top	It's just too much! (Hiring a live band and a team of juggling chimpanzees for your child's birthday would be *over the top*.)
I'm *up in the air*	I just don't know what my final decision will be.
Get it *off your chest*	Don't keep it in; just tell me what's bothering you so you can move on with your life.

Idiom, Saying, Expression	Meaning
The jury is still out	We don't know what's going to happen. We don't know how it will end.
over the hill	If you're *over the hill*, you're past the age of usefulness.
over his head	If it's *over his head*, he isn't capable of understanding it.
on the fritz	not working at the present time
What's the *lowdown*?	What is going on? What did you find out? What's the plan?
I couldn't get a *foot in the door*	I couldn't even get her to listen to me.
a drop in the bucket	not enough to make a difference
That's a *slippery slope*	If you start something you might not be able to stop.
That's a *piece of cake*!	That's easy!
toe the line	If you *toe the line*, you follow the rules very strictly.
fall through the cracks	If something *falls through the cracks*, it doesn't get taken care of.
at the end of the day	After all is said and done, this is the situation.
I'm at the *end of my rope*	I can't deal with this anymore; I don't know what to do!
get off on the wrong foot	If two people *get off on the wrong foot*, they have had a misunderstanding; perhaps one of them has said something to offend the other.
You *put your foot in your mouth*	If you've put your *foot in your mouth*, you've said something embarrassing or something you shouldn't have said.
We'll cross that bridge when we get to it	We will not worry about it until it happens.
Don't *burn your bridges*	If you make an enemy, you might be sorry later when you need him.
feet to the fire	If you hold someone's feet to the fire, you make him do what he's supposed to do.
not out of the woods yet	The danger is not over yet; the problem has not been solved.

IRREGULAR VERBS

Verb	Past Tense	Form with Helping Verbs (have, should have, will have, etc.)
be	was, were	been
blow	blew	blown
break	broke	broken
choose	chose	chosen
come	came	come
dive	dove, dived	dived
do	did	done
drink	drank	drunk
drive	drove	driven
eat	ate	eaten
fall	fell	fallen
fly	flew	flown
forgive	forgave	forgiven
get	got	gotten
give	gave	given
go	went	gone
grow	grew	grown
know	knew	known
lay	laid	laid
lie	lay	lain
ride	rode	ridden
ring	rang	rung
rise	rose	risen
run	ran	run
see	saw	seen
show	showed	shown
sing	sang	sung
sink	sank, sunk	sunk
speak	spoke	spoken
stink	stank, stunk	stunk
swim	swam	swum
take	took	taken

Verb	Past Tense	Form with Helping Verbs (have, should have, will have, etc.)
tear	tore	torn
throw	threw	thrown
wake	woke, waked	woken, waked
wear	wore	worn
weave	wove	woven
write	wrote	written

MORAL/ETHICAL VOCABULARY

Nouns

ageism	intimidation
anger	introspection
atonement	justice
avarice (greed)	legacy
bullying	loyalty
civility	metacognition
commitment	mindfulness
community	modesty
compassion	nature
conservation	patience
consideration	peace
cooperation	penance
courage	perspective
courteousness	philanthropy
decency	prejudice
deception	pride
discrimination	privilege
empathy	privacy
envy	progeny
ethics	progress
fairness	racism

faith
forgiveness
freedom
friendship
generosity
gentleness
grace
gratitude
greed
grief
guilt
happiness
hate
honesty
hubris
humiliation
humility
hypocrisy
indifference
innocence lost
integrity
interdependence

reciprocity
recompense
reflection
respect
responsibility
restitution
revenge
rights
sacrifice
sacrilege
self-control
selfishness
selflessness
sexism
shame
sloth
solitude
spirit
support
tolerance
trust
vengeance

Adjectives

careless
circumspect
conflicted
egalitarian

equitable
meditative
non-judgmental
open

Verbs

allow
care

promise
question

consider	rectify
console	restore
listen	sacrifice
nourish	share
opine (think)	understand

MULTIPLE-MEANING WORDS

When students are made aware of the various meanings of words such as these, they enjoy incorporating them into humorous, or serious, vignettes.

arm	mark
back	move
balance	off
bear	on
beat	open
break	order
call	over
case	part
catch	pass
charge	pitch
clean	place
clear	plant
cross	play
cover	point
draft	post
draw	reach
drive	run
even	scale
face	see
fair	set
fall	show
fast	shoot
field	sign

figure	sink
fine	spell
fit	stand
fix	step
fly	strike
foot	table
go	tap
head	take
high	tender
hit	throw
light	tie
line	tip
make	work

POWERFUL VERBS

Other Ways to Say "Went"

ambled	retreated
backpedaled	rocketed
barreled	rolled
blew	rushed
bolted	sashayed
bounced	sauntered
brushed	scrambled
budged	shot
catapulted	shoved
clambered	shuffled
clawed	sidled
crawled	skated
crept	skedaddled
danced	skipped
darted	skittered

dashed	skulked
dodged	slalomed
dragged	slid
drifted	slipped
edged	slithered
elbowed	slunk
feinted	snaked
felt (his way)	sneaked, snuck
flew	sped
floated	spun
galloped	staggered
galumphed	stalked
glided	stepped
greased	stole
hobbled	stomped
hopped	stormed
hurried	strode
hustled	strutted
inched	stumbled
jumped	tiptoed
launched	toddled
limped	traipsed
lunged	tramped
lurched	trekked
made (her way)	tripped
marched	tromped
meandered	trotted
moved	trudged
muscled	tumbled
paddled	vaulted
pivoted	waddled
plodded	waded

plowed   walked
plunged   wandered
pranced   weaved
propelled   wobbled
pushed   wormed
raced   zigzagged
ran   zipped
rappelled   zoomed

Other Ways to Say "Said"

acknowledged   ordered
admitted   pestered
agreed   pleaded
barked   pressed
cautioned   pried
conceded   probed
confessed   purred
confirmed   quipped
corrected   repeated
declared   retorted
demanded   scolded
exclaimed   screamed
explained   screeched
gasped   shot back
groaned   sighed
groused   snapped
growled   snickered
grumbled   sputtered
grunted   stammered
hissed   stuttered
huffed   suggested
insinuated   teased

insisted	threatened
interjected	warned
interrupted	whimpered
joked	whined
laughed	whispered
lied	wondered aloud
mentioned	yammered
mumbled	yelled
murmured	yelped
offered	yipped

PERSUASIVE ESSAY TOPICS

Kids Philosophy Slam Topics

- Which is more powerful, love or hate?
- Truth or beauty, which has a greater impact on society?
- Which is more important in your life, truth or beauty?
- Which has a greater impact on society, violence or compassion?
- Imagination or knowledge, which has a greater impact on society?
- Do the ends justify the means?
- Is the pen mightier than the sword?
- Greed or giving, which has a greater impact on society?
- Is global warming the greatest challenge facing humankind?
- Which is more powerful, hope or fear?
- War or peace: Is world peace possible, or does human nature make war inevitable?
- Is the nature of humankind good or evil?
- What is the meaning of life? (This is the only *open-ended* KPS question.)

Author-Generated Topics

- Are technical advances always a good thing?
- Should we establish a flat income tax rate of 10 percent for everyone?
- Does our genetic makeup *or* our upbringing determine our behavior?
- Does education determine your success in life?
- Why do bullies bully?
- Should capital punishment be outlawed in the United States?
- Should the legal voting age be lowered to 16?

Bibliography

Dillard, Annie. *The Writing Life*. New York: Harper Perennial, 1998.
Driscoll, Michael, illustrated by Meredith Hamilton. *A Child's Introduction to Poetry*. New York: Black Dog & Leventhal, 2003.
Goldberg, Natalie. *Writing Down the Bones: Freeing the Writer Within*. Boston: Shambhala Publications, 1986, 2005.
Graves, Donald H. *Writing: Teachers & Children at Work*. Portsmouth, NH: Heinemann Educational Books, 1983.
Holtan, Thea. *Think, Organize, Write! The Thinking and Writing Process*. St. Paul, MN: Thea-Thot Press, 2002.
Lamott, Anne. *Bird by Bird: Some Instructions on Writing and Life*. New York: Anchor Books, 1994.
Lane, Barry. *After the End: Teaching and Learning Creative Revision*. Portsmouth, NH: Heinemann, 1993.
Lucas, Stephen E., and Martin J. Medhurst. *Words of a Century: The Top 100 American Speeches, 1900–1999*. Oxford: Oxford University Press, 2008.
McCourt, Frank. *Teacher Man*. New York: Scribner, 2005.
Spalding, Romalda Bishop, edited by Mary E. North. *The Writing Road to Reading: The Spalding Method for Teaching Speech, Spelling, Writing, and Reading*. 6th edition. New York: HarperCollins, 2012.
Thurber, James. "The Secret Life of Walter Mitty." *New Yorker*, March 18, 1939.
Ueland, Brenda. *If You Want to Write: A Book about Art, Independence and Spirit*. St. Paul, MN: Graywolf Press, 2007.
University of Chicago Press. *The Chicago Manual of Style*. 16th edition. Chicago: University of Chicago Press, 2010.

www.ingramcontent.com/pod-product-compliance
Lightning Source LLC
Chambersburg PA
CBHW021848300426
44115CB00005B/68